For Marie
enjoy

THROUGH
MY EYES

The Journal of
Belle Munro
(Saskatoon 1908 to 1918)

by
Margaret Munro

Margaret Munro

 FriesenPress

One Printers Way
Altona, MB R0G 0B0
Canada

www.friesenpress.com

ISBN
978-1-03-916400-0 (Hardcover)
978-1-03-916399-7 (Paperback)
978-1-03-916401-7 (eBook)

1. BIOGRAPHY & AUTOBIOGRAPHY, PERSONAL MEMOIRS

Distributed to the trade by The Ingram Book Company

Table of Contents

Belle and Arch Munro, 1893

YOU ARE REMEMBERED

Belle and Archie Munro
Their children
George, Helen, Nan
Jim, Hugh and Bill (my father)
and
Nancy Jill Stobbe
1960 – 2012

Scattered Thoughts
of the Author – 2022

Being of considerable age, I wondered what I could possibly do during the long Covid-19 pandemic. I live alone and I knew I would soon tire of my own company.

Seniors are often cautioned not to live in the past; however, living in the present, especially nowadays, is not much fun and the future is uncertain.

Margaret Munro … contemplating the history
of her family and city.

I decided to write about the past. The past I chose to
visit was not my own, but the lives of Belle and Archie
Munro. In the form of her journal, I attempt to tell
Belle's story. The family came to Saskatoon in 1908.
Through her eyes, I tell the story of Saskatoon. Facts
about Saskatoon have been well researched. All the
names of the people are real. The sources come from
oral family stories and the internet. Terry Hokness of
Saskatoon has read, scanned and posted over 80,500

items gleaned from Saskatoon newspaper. His work helped make mine possible.

The letters sent to Belle from Arch in 1907 and the WWI letters sent from Hugh and Bill Munro to their parents in Saskatoon are as presented. These letters were preserved by my sister, Win (Munro) Parker.

A note of explanation on style is needed. This book takes the form of the diaries of Belle Munro as imagined by me. Part of this imagining is reflected in the form. Belle was an intelligent, articulate, educated woman – but she would have written any diaries for her own eyes. She would have made some grammatical and spelling errors. Some things would not have been presented in a linear narrative. As I've imagined her diary, I've also tried to imagine the kind of "errors" she would have made (that is, errors to a modern, professional copy editor) and present them to you. I believe this diary is as she would have written it.

My "moonlight" years have been brightened by my two sons, Earl and Mark Stobbe. Thanks for respecting me, encouraging me and loving me.

My two grandsons, Jake and Nick Stobbe always bring me joy and happiness. They are my sunshine.

On completion of this hand printed manuscript, I was stymied how to proceed. I doubt if this book would have come to fruition if my cousin Nan Zorn had not offered to put it in a printable form. Her enthusiasm and affirmation mean a lot to me. Nan is the youngest grandchild of Belle Munro and of the nine grandchildren, she is most like our grandmother. Thank you, Nan.

I promised my two great-granddaughters, Emma and Lily, that their names would appear in this book. Your enthusiasm for life and learning gives me hope for the future. Along with your cousins Magnus, Miles, Fiona and Ilyana and your third cousins Clara and Simon, keep and record the family stories. Just as my story (I hope) helps shape your journey, remember to leave accounts of your paths for next generations.

Here is a verse that was popular to write in autograph books 100 years ago:

> Life is like a path
> Of freshly driven snow.
> Be careful how you tread it,
> For every step will show.

This is my verse I write in your "autograph books".

March to the future, bravely and bold,
Yet live every day with laughter and love.

Once in a while – stop – look back to your ancestors and envision them as they were. They stumbled and fell but got back up to finish their adventures. You are their "gold". Pass it on!

Hope, joy, peace and love to all those who travel back in time with me.

Margaret (Mugs) Munro

1908

June 1908

I am beyond excitement! Last Wednesday we moved into our new house at 422 Ninth Street in Nutana.

Arch was with us in Prince Albert to help us pack. He made arrangements to have all our furniture and goods shipped by train to Saskatoon. He was a passenger on the same train so he could keep an eye on our belongings. He hired the Saskatoon Forwarding Co. to take our belongings to the house. The company provided two men to do the carrying and lifting and they helped him set up all the beds.

The children and I stayed 3 nights in a hotel in P.A. and then caught the train to Saskatoon all by ourselves. I must say I couldn't have managed without Willie and Hugh. Willie, almost 13, stepped forward and bravely asked lots of questions. We should have sent more with the furniture, but both boys managed most of the luggage we had with us.

All the children were excited by the trip on the train. I think Jim is going to be like Willie as he asked endless questions, sometimes to my embarrassment.

Arch met us at the train and hired the newly formed Union Bus to deliver us to our front door.

After quickly exploring the house from basement to attic, all six children announced they were hungry. Before I could even think what to serve, Arch produced four cans of tomato soup and made a cup of tea. He had also bought two loaves of fresh bread from Booth's Bakery and some peanut butter. He had bought most of the staples and, of course, a full line of Blue Ribbon spices, baking powder and tea.

Arch is such a dear! After the soup and bread had been devoured, he produced a large sack of Barnum's Animal Crackers, Geordie's favourite cookie. The three older boys should have had larger cookies, as soon Willie was challenging Hugh and Jim to see who could stuff the most animals in their mouths at one time. Arch declared Jim won, then shut down the fun by removing the bag of cookies. After supper, we had to sort out the bedrooms. There is a large square bedroom at the front of the house. Arch had our bedroom furniture set up there.

The second bedroom also faces the front to the North. He had set up a double bed there. The third bedroom, a little smaller, also has a double bed. After some discussion, we decided that Hugh and Jim would be in the front room and the folding cot for Geordie has been added.

The fourth bedroom is very small and has no closet. I wanted it for a sewing room and a single bed when Mother comes to visit. Willie had other plans. He desperately wants his own room, so we are allowing him that – if he shares it with my sewing and if he will bunk in with the boys with no complaining when Grannie Stewart comes to visit. Hugh put up a good front, but he has always shared with Willie. He will need patience with Jim, who sometimes is annoying. The girls will share the back bedroom.

And, of course, the bathroom! A flush toilet and hot (if we heat it) and cold water faucets. Geordie and Helen thought it was fun to flush the toilet, but we soon put an end to that!

422 Ninth Street East in Saskatoon – 114 years after Belle Munro first laid eyes on her new home.

Our house looks very fine on the outside. It is a full two-story with an attic that has three dormer windows. The icing on the cake, as far as I am concerned, is a square centre with a decorative railing. I think this space could be made into a very large room, but for now we will just use it for storage.

When a person enters through the front door, there is a long hall right through to the kitchen. On the right is a pleasant staircase to the second floor. On the left, pretty French doors open to the parlour. There are pocket doors between the parlour and dining room. The dining room is also accessed by a door from the kitchen.

The basement! The little ones are timid about going to the basement. There is a large, forced air furnace with shiny pipes leading to places upstairs. In winter this furnace heats the water we need. In summer when we do not use the furnace, there is a little wee stove, called a jacket heater. A small fire easily heats the water tank.

In the corner near the furnace is an area fenced off. Imagine – we have a chute from outside. Coal and wood go down directly and land in the fenced off section. If we have a cord of wood delivers, the boys' job will be to scramble into the fenced area and throw the wood onto the floor before chopping it. Willie is so excited as he doesn't have to chop wood outside anymore. All done, it is a cozy warm basement.

My kitchen – where to start! There is new congoleum on the floor. They chose a nice modern pattern – checks of blue and tan. Also, there is a new coal and wood range that has a warming oven and a reservoir. The nice large kitchen sink is enclosed and has a good countertop attached to it. We brought two storage cupboards with us and they are painted white, as are our kitchen table and chairs. We have a white bench at the back of the table into which at least three of the children can slide. I'm glad our six chairs are square and rather compact so three of the chairs fit on the other side and then a chair at each end. The sixth chair is up in the bathroom. I will buy a blue oilcloth for the table and sew new blue curtains that can be drawn at night. I brought my Hoosier. On the upper left, it has a proper flour bin and sifter. Inside the cupboard doors to the upper right, I keep all my baking goods. I love that it also has an area to keep bread and pies. This is closed with little folding doors.

The countertop part is enamel that can be pulled out when baking. Pots and pans fit into the two large cupboards at the bottom. We keep dishes in our white cupboards. Nan suggested we store cups and bowls on the lower shelves so they can all reach them. For many years I have had to keep things high so babies would not destroy them.

Our first Saturday night here. Arch fired up the jacket heater soon there was hot water for bathing. We usually bathed Helen and Nan together and thought they would like to bath separately. Instead, they wanted to enjoy the fun together and Nan pointed out that they should have double the water!

Geordie was fascinated, pulling the plug and watching the water swirl away. Then he would say "Geordie's not finished and want more water!"

Our first Sunday morning at 422! All the Sunday clothes were ready. We both are so proud of our family. When Arch is home, we always have a scripture and then a prayer (sometimes very lengthy). Arch, for the scripture reading today, chose Joshua 24, verse 2: "As for me and my house, we will serve God."

Arch then questions each child to say something about what they have just heard. He always starts with Willie and sometimes his comment is not quite what his father anticipated and his answer leaves Arch in a quandary as to approve Willie's statement, ignore it or to argue about it. Hugh always works in his standard – either God loves us, or we love God. That seems to satisfy Arch. Jim often takes Willie's statement but rephrases it so it pleases his Dad. (We think Jim might be a good minister someday.) The girls usually repeat the phrase that Hugh offered.

Now we have all started to worry about wee Geordie. He Is 3 ½ and never refers to himself as 'I'. He just copies the others and says, "Geordie likes cookies" instead of "I like cookies."

Finally, Arch turned to Geordie. Geordie replied, "As for me and my house, we will serve God". Arch was beaming. Then he asked Geordie if he would like porridge for breakfast. Geordie replied in a deep, clear voice, "As for me and my house – yes, please!" The other children thought this was so funny, so they started to pepper him with questions. He started every answer with "As for me and my house". Of course, he knew it brought laugher. I wonder how long he will reply this way. To me, I think Geordie loves his house the most.

After breakfast, we set out to walk over the new bridge to Knox Presbyterian Church. It is not a huge, impressive brick church such as are in the big cities, but a simple wood on the pretty riverbank. The Church was filled to overflowing. with a lot of single men and a lot that rolled their "rrr's".

Tears came to my eyes when the congregation rose and sang

Holy, holy, holy, Lord God Almighty
Early in the morning
Our song shall rise to thee

I closed my eyes and thought of the churches of my youth, in Ottawa and Winnipeg areas. I feel we are truly home after several years of uncertainty. Of course, we sang "All people that on earth do dwell" – The Old 100th.

The minister preached a fine sermon, emphasizing how God gave us such blessings to live in Canada and in Saskatoon. After the offering was collected, we sang "Praise God from whom all blessings flow". Outside after the service, Arch met several people that he knew and introduced us proudly.

The little ones were getting tired on the long walk home, so they did not go to Sunday School. Arch wanted to walk the three boys back to Sunday School, but Willie said if his Dad came along, he would not go! Arch is very social and looked forward to seeing the set up for Sabbath School, but he stayed home. Willie is a long like his father, very friendly and outgoing but I think their likeness leads to some head butting.

The next thing to set up was how I would wash clothes.

I have a double tub stand that folds up. We store it in the basement along with the two tubs and wringer. The boys get it up for me to the kitchen, usually on Mondays. No more carrying pails of water outside, just empty into the kitchen sink!

I love my clotheslines. Luckily the Schmidts set up a good system. I have one pulley line, but Schmidt got sturdy poles and supports from his farm and built one with six lines. I have to walk along and pin clothes on them, but this is the best setup I have ever had. Next spring, we want to plant grass under them. If it rains, it is a little muddy now. I imagine it will be well used by the girls to play under. A blanket thrown over the lines will give them a shady place to play.

Dr. McKay cautions us to boil drinking and cooking water because of typhoid fever.

I wanted to set up a system with two large crocks, one with a spout, so everyone can help themselves. The other crock, with a dipper, is for cooking water. I wanted a special table built to hold both crocks. Arch isn't much of a carpenter, so I drew up exact plans with accurate measurements. He took my plans to the lumber company just a block away. I told him to ask them to saw the boards according to my measurements.

There is a small extra fee, on top of the material, for cutting the parts. The plan was that Arch could nail them together. Arch turned on his charm and said how he didn't know how to assemble it. The upshot was that the many offered to put it together for an extra dollar. Arch was very happy! He and Willie brought it home with our wagon.

Nan had suggested building a lower shelf under the crock part. It was a great idea, as we now each keep a cup on the shelf. Sometimes Geordie needs a little help, but it is much handier. The girls' job is to put a clean teacloth on the shelf every few days and wash all the cups. Maybe I am fussy, but I always hated to see everyone drinking from a common dipper. Every time I have the stove lit, I boil kettles of water for 20 minutes, cool the water and then add it to the crocks. We are going to paint this water table white, as well as the wood box near the stove.

I have a large icebox. I set it up near the kitchen door, so the iceman doesn't have to track up the whole floor. We have the iceman deliver a block of ice every Friday and Tuesday. Dr. McKay is warning about chipping off chunks of ice for drinks, as the ice is frozen river water – the source of typhoid. We have assigned Hugh and Jim to empty the pan under the icebox.

Arch is back on the road. I am glad it is summer as there is no school until fall. I could not have managed without the help of Willie and Hugh. Willie is really growing – about his father's height, while Hugh is very slight. The girls have taken over Geordie, so he not so clingy to me. Jim floats between being with his older brothers or he plays well with the girls. I think he is a leader like Willie and not such a good follower, so, with the younger ones, he takes charge. He loves playing with the girls' paper dolls. He adds things like paper floor plans, roads and houses.

Partly as a joke, and partly with a purpose in mind, Arch bought Willie a brand new spade. Arch painted his initials on it. Then Hugh was presented with a fork, also with initials. Jim got a new rake. The purpose was to get a garden dug and spaded. Willie is going to be paid 10¢ an hour. Hugh will get 9¢ and the raker, Jim, will earn 8¢ an hour. Nan and Helen are given sacks and they get 2¢ for each sack full of weeds they pick.

We are rushing to plant potatoes. They will be late, but even if we get a few, it would be good. I teased Arch that I was getting him a brand new hoe to hill the potatoes, but he says our old one is good and fits well in my hands. Willie and Hugh want to earn money so they can go to the exhibition.

July 1908

July 1st was Willie's 13th birthday! It seems only yesterday he was born – a bonny boy with a large, well-rounded head with eyes that seemed to change from blue to grey.

Since then, 13 years ago, I have had 5 more children, we moved 5 times, had a business, then sold it and now Arch is on a new venture! (I was 30 when Willie was born and almost 40 when Geordie was born. Now I am glad I did not get married at 18 because I could have had 9 or 10 more children!)

For a birthday present we got him a new bicycle – a brand new Standard Gent's Model. It is still a little heavy for him, but he can manage. It's too heavy for Hugh.

We got him the four volume Johnathan Swift's 'Gulliver's Travels' as he likes long books. Of course, there was chocolate cake – his favourite – with 13 candles.

Birthday time again! July 4th we celebrated Jim's birthday. We gave him a new baseball bat, ball and glove. The boys are starting to play more in the empty lot beside our house. They keep the lot fairly clean and cut back the weeds and grass. It is good we don't have windows on that side of the house. Because it was so hot, Jim got to start his special day with his favourite cold cereal, Shredded Wheat. I made a salad with my dressing I make. We had generous slices of fresh bread (bought, as it was too warm to put the stove on).

Instead of cake we had one of Jim's favourites. I made chocolate icing, then put it between layers of graham crackers. Then they can be cut as bars through the layers. The candle was an ordinary candle. I put it in a little dish in the centre of a large plate, then piled cut pieces all around it in a decorative fashion. A huge pitcher of lemonade was welcome in the heat. Jim's book was 'The Treasure Seekers' by Nesbitt.

August 1908

Our first summer is almost over! I am glad I had Willie and Hugh to be my eyes of the town. I have noticed since after Geordie was born, I have slowed down on what I can do! I find the heat of summer too much.

Willie was fascinated that the houses on Broadway do not have "house" numbers like some of the older residences do. So, he took a pencil and paper and one of Arch's hand clipboards and decided to make me a listing and a map of Broadway. When he finished, we were all surprised about how many places there are! I think he had them memorized and when his father came home for the weekends, he showed the same keen interest. Like son, like father!

Then I discovered in a closet that the Schmidts had carefully left a neat stack of Phoenix newspapers from 1907 until we moved in. The boys decided that they would visit all the places mentioned.

It is hard to believe the changes in a year. Willie and Arch plan to study and learn the early history.

Willie's first 'port of call' was the newly built Grand Trunk Bridge. The paper said the piers would be finished by August 1907. It cost over a half a million dollars and had crews of 150 men working night and day. The boys were impressed and started their list.

The next opening was of St. James Church in 1907. They suggested we attend some Sunday to see the inside, but Anglicans and Presbyterians are far apart in theology. The Anglicans have more liturgy, similar to the Roman Catholics.

All in all, they found it was a "pretty church on the west side of the river".

The Traffic Bridge united communities on both sides of the South Saskatchewan River to make it possible to join the Saskatoon, Nutana and Riversdale into the city of Saskatoon in 1906.

One Saturday they crossed the bridge again and went into I.F. Cairns new store. They also discovered Idylwyld Park. Over on the west side of the river, they checked out the new Flanigan Hotel. They did not try to enter as they would have not gained access.

While downtown, they saw the new King Edward Hotel which had a white brick front.

I did not realize the Traffic Bridge we cross to go to church was almost brand new.

The boys wish we had moved here straight from Morden as they would have had to cross the river by ferry.

One day they walked as far as the new Princess Alexandra School which was built last year. They were disappointed as it looked like any ordinary school – nothing 'royal' about it!

Jim started to read some of the papers and he was fascinated by a report of an accident in November last year. He begged his brother to take him to the site. In a long descriptive article, it told a story that appealed to a ten year old boy. It reported that Miss Clarence and Miss Craig were driving a horse and buggy by the railroad crossing on 23rd Street on a Sunday evening. They had to wait as a long line of railway cars were being shunted back and forth. They thought the coast was finally clear and they whipped up the horse to hurry over the tracks. Too late, they saw a car shunting back. The driver used her whole strength to make the horse back up, but the horse was uncontrollable with fright and sprang ahead. The engine crashed into the buggy and the horse dragged it forward just beyond the reach of the wheel. The two women looked up and saw the train coming and both jumped out of the buggy.

After a long walk, Willie found the location and Jim was so disappointed. He expected to see broken bits of buggy, maybe horsetail hairs, or even ripped petticoats! Of course, nothing was left at the scene of an accident that happened 10 months ago.

In June, the new Court House was opened. Willie wisely chose not to go in. I teased him that they might have charged him with vagrancy! The biggest event happened just a week before we moved. The steamer 'The Medicine Hat' crashed into a pier at the new Traffic Bridge. The boat split in two and sank. People from both sides of the river still go down to the site but there is not much to see.

September 1908

School opening. I wanted our family, as newcomers, to look very smart.

The night before they had to have baths and the boys are too big for us to actually bathe them, but they had to endure a check by me. Willie was sent back to the tub to do a better job on his neck. It looked like Hugh never washed his elbows, so he had to take the brush to them. Jim's hands looked as if they had not been washed for a long time, so I did take the scrub brush to his knuckles.

Nan was her usual clean, sweet smiling self. (I'm glad I had two girls, so I know how different they are from boys.)

The three boys had new knickers and long socks. They also had brand new pullover sweaters. I am going to get Willie one more on sale, as he has outgrown his other ones, which are passed down to Hugh. And Hugh's go to Jim. Nan had a new gingham dress and I am going sew her two more of heavier fabric. She got a pretty new sweater jacket.

Of course, Willie and Hugh were supposed to shepherd the others. They were instructed to go straight down 9th Street to Broadway and then down about three blocks to school.

After a couple of days, I was puzzled about how dusty Nan's skirt was. It turns out that Willie found a shortcut down the back lane past the barn to come out at Broadway by the Garrison House, now the first hotel in Nutana. Arch pointed out that even if we insisted, they would take the shortcut. The two older boys will go that way. It is time that Jim becomes a little more responsible at 10 years, so he was instructed to walk Nan the proper way. He is such a dear, he did not look on it as punishment because he and Nan are good friends. Also, Jim loves to be in charge!

School opened and all four children are happy with their teachers. However, it took about two weeks to get everything settled. Helen is going to be home another year, as her birthday is November.

Imagine! At Victoria school they planned for an increase. The had 90 pupils on the roll. Ours were included in this number as Arch went in the summer to let them know they would be adding four more. 140 showed up! They rented space in the Butler Building and moved about 50 high school pupils there. I am glad Willie was not in high school as that is a ling hike twice a day! In anticipation of a new high school, they hired Archibald Mather as Principal at $1,200 a year. The School Board had closed the original stone schoolhouse built in 1887 and the plans were to tear it down. But this fall, they had to reopen it and place two senior rooms there. So even though it was the oldest school in the city, Willie was they only one in the family to be in there. However, the School Board, looking ahead, knew they would be short of desks and ordered new single seat desks, more suited to older children.

In February, the Government of Saskatchewan ordered a new set of readers. There are five books in the series, from a primer and four more levels. Nan and Jim are excited as the readers are fresh and have new material. All the boys had the older ones memorized to the point that Hugh would say a page number and the rest would recite the contents of the page. Some children had the pages memorized even though they couldn't recognize those words in another book – so they really couldn't read. The new readers encourage pupils to learn sounds and actually figure out words on their own.

Of interest, school enrolments and teachers were listed.

Year	Pupils	Teachers
1902	112	2
1903	136	3
1904	158	4
1905	213	5
1906	296	6
1907	364	10
1908	651 (est)	16

No wonder the School Board is scrambling!

Dr McKay was right as usual! Typhoid and smallpox are always with us. In early September Mr. Pulsford, his wife and three daughters died from typhoid. Two sons are still in hospital. Also, in Halbrite, there was a smallpox outbreak of 13 families.

I noticed in the newspaper on September 12 how they were gouging out Victoria Hill and grading it. They reported there were nine J.D.D. scrapers working side by side.

Then I thought to ask Willie if he had ridden his bicycle over there. Sure enough, he told all about it in great detail. Arch laid the law down and he is forbidden to go where there is construction going on. Even if he is 13, accidents do happen. I reminded him of the report of the four-year-old son of Frank Booth. Workmen were hauling gravel to grade part of Fifth Avenue. Children had been getting in the wagon for rides. As the horses were making their last run before 5 p.m., the young boy was crushed by a wagon wheel.

I keep thinking – what if that had been little Geordie? It would be just terrible to lose a son of any age. That is why we don't let the three little ones go anywhere without supervision. Horses and autos seem to have taken over the streets!

October 1908

The weather is definitely chillier.

I feel like recording the story of how we arrived her in Saskatoon.

Arch Munro and his daughter Nan in 1903.

Trying to find where we belonged took a few years. I can count our moves by where each child was born.

Willie was born in Emerson, but within the year we had moved nearby to Stockton, where Hugh was born. Jim was born in Winkler. Then we moved to Morden. Shortly after Nan was born, we bought a general store. We did very well for a few years. We rented a very nice house on the edge of town. Helen and Geordie Mack were born there.

That would have been our life, but Arch got into politics and talked openly (too much) about his political views. He learned this was a huge mistake. The ones that did not share his views slowly stopped coming to the store. When they started verbally attacking Arch as a person, Arch fell into a huge depression. I suggested that we sell the store, which we did, and made a handsome profit. Arch was coming slowly back to his old self but in the spring of 1907, we knew he had to find work.

Now, through the store connections Arch met the two Gault cousins. They had started a company in Winnipeg. They called it Blue Ribbon and had a full line of baking goods. The most popular was their baking powder.

Arch Munro

Arch often said one of his dreams had been to go west, so when Gaults wanted to hire him to scout out a good centre in Saskatchewan to expand into, he was keen to go. After much soul searching and prayer, I suggested he accept. It would be very irresponsible to take a family into the unknown, so I suggested he go alone. I said I would manage alone for three months. I could not have coped if it was for winter months. The added chores of winter, plus six children, a cow and a pony!

We wrote letters back and forth. I wish I had saved Arch's because he told of his adventures. Arch carefully saved my letters to him. They were not very interesting, but I am going to report parts of them in case anyone in the future would appreciate the struggle.

Arch's letters could have been filled with adventures, but he carefully did not stress his freedom, but rather he always wrote how much he missed us and how devoted he was to finding a good place for his family.

I am recording some of the letters I wrote to him.

June 6, 1907

Dear Arch,

I received both your letters yesterday. We are all well. Nan cried so hard the first night you were away. I had quite a time to quiet her and she seems to be lonesome. She has me nearly smashed to pieces. And Geordie is always asking for you. One morning he came and asked, "Is Daddy home?" The rest seem about as usual when you are away.

I let the three boys go to Uncle Tom's Cabin last night as they will miss the excursions to Winnipeg. I was up early and milked as Willie will have a hard day.

I have not been in the store since you left. We are very lonely and there does seem so many things to see to. If we had only thoroughly cleaned the cellar before you left. We have any amount of soft water.

Willie has gone to the store. The rest of the children are just getting up and there is a great hubbub. The boys are good and very interested in letters you have written to them. Helen says she thinks you will find us a house.

It grows quite windy and disagreeable. It is just splendid this morning, not a bit of wind and the air is delicious. Now the wind!

I will write again as soon as I know where to find you. You will hear from the children often.

Yours, with love, Belle

June 18, 1907

Dear Archie,

This is Sunday and one of the very hottest days we could have. We are all feeling tired from the heat. Nan answered your letter last week.

I got a cheque for $200 from Peter at the store. I shall draw it out of the Union Bank and place it in the Bank of Hamilton. Willie will come with me tomorrow.

The children are just in from Sunday School. They are very warm. I did not let Helen go.

On Friday I washed my blankets and curtains and got up at half past four on Saturday. I have found a good washer woman who promises to come every two weeks, so I won't have to work so hard after this. I have always got up and milked Saturdays and Sundays, so Willie can sleep. On weekdays he is up at half six – then Walter takes the cow at seven to the pasture.

Everyone wants to know when you are coming home. What do you think of the new towns you are passing through? I found a pair of Waghorn maps and we follow you on the maps. Billy is threatening to cut the boys' hair.

I wish I could see you. Three months is a long time to be a widow.

Morden June 26, 1907

Dear Arch,

I just received your letter written from Edmonton yesterday. Brother Donald was out here preaching in church on Sunday. I had to hustle home to make dinner. His sermons were enjoyable. A number of people here who normally do not go to church came out. His visit did us all good. I wish it had been longer. He will write to you about it and the fuss the kiddies made over him.

I have finished my hardest work and I am sewing. My washer woman has let me down and so I am getting Rosy Boulton to help me sew. I can't do everything, but I would rather sew.

Hugh wants to write to you tonight. He is a little disappointed as he expected his second letter, but he did not say anything. He was quite pleased that Nan got one.

Poor Geordie is asleep. He runs to Mrs. Flors quite often. I had to punish him several times. Jim had a tooth pulled yesterday.

Must close now with love to you from all the kiddies as well as myself.

Belle

Geordie Munro in Morden, Manitoba – 1906.

Morden June 30, 1907

Dear Arch,

Sunday afternoon and five children are off to Church School. Geordie is asleep upstairs and the house seems very empty. I wish, wherever you are, you could drop in for a couple of hours anyway to brighten up the week.

Tomorrow will be a holiday. The children will be home for the summer.

I have not felt very well for a few days. I am trying to take things easier and will not work nearly so hard. I have to pay Black the rent tomorrow. I suppose we may have to pay as much for very much less house. I think we had better buy in P.A. than rent. Property is advancing everywhere. I think Billy finds Saturdays very long. I did _not_ milk for him yesterday or this morning for the first time, but after milking he went back to bed and had his sleep out.

Geordie says when you come back, he is going to get you and you won't get away! The dear little man, everybody loves him he is such a pet and he is just as good as he can be.

I must close now and make dinner.

Love, Belle

Morden July 4, 1907

At last the letters seem to be sorted out. You seem to be getting all ours. What about yours? If I had not heard in a week, I was going to wire you. I seldom go out and the children and I just look for letters.

I hope P.A. works out. I do not wish to go to Saskatoon, it would be too gay.

Mr. Andrew was inquiring about you. I told him you had lost ten pounds. We do not eat as much meat in the hot weather. Sometimes the boys think we are not overfed, but in hot weather we do not need meat.

Willie was quite disappointed that you did not write him on his birthday. He had a big feed and got a lacrosse stick that he has been wanting. The two boys went with Walter last night to swim. The boys are good, but they are getting pretty headstrong about some things and scrap from morning till night. They have slept outside several times this month.

We always pray for you, for everything that you do, you may be protected from every harm and danger of every kind, and I am glad you have given over your care to the place it belongs.

I find it hard not to carry just as much of the load I can carry and I am afraid that I only lay it down when I can't help myself. The children always pray for you and long so for you to be home.

Do you think the boys should have the horse to drive? Twice Willie had her and he went to Kerr's both times and stayed much longer than he should have. I told him I would ask you and see what you said about it.

Have you got your certificate for your own shares in the Silver Leaf mine? I can't find them.

I must close now; it is very late.

> With very best, love from
> your loving wife. Belle

July 7

Jim had his birthday. He got up early and took the cow to pasture. Willie got stingy and decided to take the cow to pasture this summer. He gets the 50 ¢ a month we paid to hire. Then he tricks his brothers into getting the cow. Jim was thrilled to do it all alone on his 9th birthday. Then Helen and Geordie took some milk to Mrs. Sutherland all by themselves.

We had a good long sing this morning – the children all enjoy it. Willie wants me to ask you if he can ride the horse sometime if Walter gets it ready.

I must close now with bushels of love.

Belle

***

July 10, 1907

Dear Arch

A bundle of mail arrived this morning and it was very welcome. The children have been so pleased with their cards and letters.

Mrs. McLeod came over yesterday and found me not well and she wanted to take the three little ones home but I would not let her. Word spread and in the evening, Mrs. Andrew called and Mrs. Sutherland and Bea Ainsley came over and brought some brandy, so I had a houseful.

The children are very good, only like children they forget sometimes and are a bit thoughtless.

I hope it won't be long until we have a business of our own and can work together.

The boys think it would be great to be able to help — especially travelling.

Sister Maggie and Enoch were to leave on their trip Monday morning. Mother is coming out the end of this week?

I have both accident insurance policies together and will keep them safe.

Willie will write soon.

Lovingly, Belle

On October 10th we celebrated Georgie's 4th birthday. We probably should have made more fuss, but he is still young enough not to notice. We tend to buy him toys that are a little too young for him whereas the older boys we tend to push ahead more.

Geordie had seen a picture of a Steiff bear on wheels, so that is what we got him. He loves putting all the other stuffed animals on the bear's back and pulling them around. The girls' dolls are off limits to him. Yes, he is talking more and is using his imagination

– AND he says "I" and has given up the "As for me and my house".

All in all, he is a delightful child and the perfect fit to be number 6. He is four and I thought there might be a number 7 about two years ago. I am pretty sure, as the years go on – there will not be more 'little Arches' nor tiny 'Belles'.

November 1908

I need to go back and tell the story now we got to Saskatoon earlier this year. In late July 1907 Arch was setting up in P.A.

We moved from Morden lock, stock and barrel, minus our horse and cow. We rented a house on the east flats near a school for the children.

Here is an entry from my old journal in February 1908:

"I hate it here. The winter is long and harsh and Arch is away a lot. Also, some of the children always seem to be sick. Arch is trying to establish his route, however several lumber camps around P.A. like his product, but he has to hitch a ride or hire someone with a horse and sleigh. This town is very rough. It is older than Saskatoon but is built on lumber and mills."

In the early months of 1908, I knew I could not continue here. I admit I sulked, cried and complained until Arch wrote the Company to move the branch to Saskatoon. He knew enough to list solid reasons – not because he had an unhappy wife!

His reasons: 1. Saskatoon had more surrounding country villages and little stores. 2. The stores were closer together. 3. Saskatoon was the hub of trade and commerce. 4. People were spending more money. The Company agreed.

Arch went down to Saskatoon to buy a house. He was talking to a store owner in Nutana who said there was a fine new house on 9th Street for sale. There were only two houses on the street but the way the town was growing there was sure to be more added. He contacted the owner, Mr. Schmidt and offered him $1,400. Mr. Schmidt jumped, so we knew he made a profit. Archie said he did not ask nor care what Mr. Schmidt had paid. Of course, there are some who say we paid too much.

It was a fine deal as Mr. Schmidt had had the house for a year and was a handyman and during the year added little things that Arch would never have got around to or would do them poorly.

The sale included a fine new kitchen stove and new congoleum in the kitchen. He set up a jacket heater in the basement. He built a sturdy bin for coal and wood that was put down a chute. In the far corner away from the furnace, he built a cold room with plenty of shelves and storage for potatoes, carrots and onions.

We were not the first family to live in it, but we always think of it as brand new.

I want to record the history of 422. Mr. Schmidt did not build the house but bought it from Mr. Kittle who built it in the fall of 1907.

In 1903 the OHR Co. (Oster, Hammond and Nanton) bought a lot of properties in Nutana for speculation. Unimproved lots, mainly on 10th, 11th and 12th Streets were selling for $10 - $15 each. Three years later the unimproved lot was sold for $300: Block 58 Lot 13. In 1907 W. Kittle built the house for speculation and quickly sold it to Mr. Schmidt, a farmer who lives just north of town, who moved into the house for the winter intending to sell it for profit later. His daughter, Lulu is Hugh's age and Bruno is the same grade as Jim.

Here we are to the end of November. We had a small party for Helen who turned 6. We bought her a deluxe wicker doll carriage with steel axles. It is so nice to have a new sidewalk. In the spring the girls are allowed up and down, but I will not let them go further afield by themselves.

Her book was 'The Tale of Mrs. Tiggy-Winkle' by Beatrix Potter. We also bought 'Peter Rabbit' but that will be saved for a Christmas present. She is starting to read as Nan comes home and teaches her. A few years ago I started a tradition with Willie. He was turning 8 in 1903 and already he had to take on so much, so I said no one could ask him to do any task that day. His brothers had to fulfill any of his wishes as long as they weren't dangerous. For example, Willie could say to Hugh "Get me a cup of water." Also, they did not have to do their assigned chores.

It has always been good fun over the years. The thing that touched me was when I couldn't ask him to do something, he always made a point of doing one thing without me hinting or asking. On each of the other children's birthdays, Willie always whispered "Offer to do something for mother." This year, Helen is full of spunk, so she thought of so many things to get her brothers to do. She had them running up and down stairs. Now her normal assigned chore is to dry the supper dishes. I thought for sure she would hand it over to Hugh, but she claimed she loved drying dishes.

I haven't written for a while but spend time sewing and getting ready for Christmas – our first at 422. We are going to do lots of decorating – paper chains being the most popular. I look forward to 1909 with a renewed sense of anticipation and joy. God has been very good to us this year.

1909

Monday January 4, 1909

Archie, the organizer, had a great practical idea! It came about because of the confusion of what books we had already and which we had given to each child. He bought a long five shelf bookcase. We set it up in the corner of the parlour, behind the big chair. The project for the children was to organize all the books we have. The easiest books were put on the bottom shelf and then up to the top shelves for adult books. Besides deciding which books should be on each shelf, the three oldest were surprised how many adult books we have and are looking forward to reading them.

These are the books we gave this past Christmas. Willie got Scottish Chiefs. It is a history of Scotland. Hugh's book is The Red Romance – 20 tales of knights. Jim got The Railway Children by Edith Nesbit. We gave Nan Elsie Dinsmore and Helen, Adventures in

Wonderland Retold. Geordie got another book by Beatrix Potter – The Tale of Jeremy Fisher.

I had read sister Maggie's copy of Glengarry School Days by Ralph Connor but want my own copy. I am intrigued that the school master's name was Archie Munro.

For Arch, I managed to get a copy of The Life of James Robertson – First Superintendent of Western Missions. It was written by a Presbyterian Minister, Charles Gordon, who also writes as Ralph Connor.

Tuesday January 5, 1909

Arch left this morning. Here is my report of the festive season.

The Scottish way is not to make too big a fuss over Christmas. After all, it is a religious holiday. These days people are making it into a gift-focused day. We decided, instead of a lot of presents at Christmas, we will make each child's birthday a special day and save presents for then.

However, each child is given a special item of clothing. I made Nan and Helen new dresses. I chose a blue fabric. They feel they are too old for smocked dresses, but older girls like sashes at the waist band. The girls loved them, and I got them each a lovely bow for their hair. Luckily their warm woolen socks and boots still fit.

The three older boys got new, bought woolen pullovers and wee Geordie Mack was happy with new knickers and stockings. They are good children and never complain if they see some of their friends get an over-abundance of toys.

I gave Arch two new neck warmers and Mocha mitts. Arch gave me a lovely shawl. McBeth's General Store had a sale. Willie took Nan to the store and the children bought me a silk handkerchief for 35 ¢. They got a set of five collars for Arch for 50 ¢!

We also get at least one new family board game. This year we bought Snakes and Ladders for the younger three and a new set of checkers so now four can play at once. Arch loves playing a good game, but he is slightly upset when Hugh wins.

Back to our special day – Hogmanay! In the Scottish tradition, we are always ready to celebrate the end of the old year and welcome in the New. We were a little downhearted as we did not know any tall dark man to be our first footer. We invited the Camerons and the Stewarts, but both these men are fair, and one has no hair!

Shortly after we moved here, we met up with Dr. William John McKay. Dr. McKay was a young doctor in Morden, Manitoba. He often came into our general store, and he was dark and handsome! Imagine our surprise to find him in Saskatoon. I did not know it, but Arch asked him to be our first footer. The children and I were so pleased when he arrived with a lump of coal for the fireplace.

Dr McKay is either adored here in Saskatoon or disliked intensely. He is trying to improve health conditions in the city. In 1906 there was a severe outbreak of typhoid. He kept preaching that this was caused by contaminated water and poor sewage. He has stressed that we must boil our drinking water, So, I always do!

Back to Hogmanay. His young wife Susanna was very nice to the girls. And the twin babies, Margaret and Hartford stole everyone's hearts. I had shortbread and black buns as well as other foods. Arch bought whiskey to toast in the New Year: "Out with the old and in with the new!" We all laughed and sang together some Burns' songs like 'The Bluebells of Scotland' and 'Flow Gently Sweet Afton'. We finished with 'Auld Lang Syne':

> "Should auld acquaintance be forgot
> And never brought to mind?

Should auld acquaintance be forgot
And the days of auld lang syne?

"For auld lang syne, my dear
For auld lang syne
We'll drink a cup of kindness yet
For the sake of auld lang syne."

Two more wonderful verses and the chorus and then we got to the best part. We crossed our arms and then gave one hand to each neighbour. Some of the children needed help, which created much laughter. As we held hands, we sang:

"And there's a hand my trusty friend
And give me a hand o' thine
We'll meet again some other night
For auld lang syne."

Then we all stepped forward to the centre of the circle and back again, with lusty cheers. Then kisses and hugs were given all around.

So, we begin the year 1909. We greet the year with hope and joy. All is right in our small world. Thanks be to God!

January 1909

The January 29th paper had an interesting story from 1884. "Chief Whitecap wanted to take the body of his son from Moose Jaw to the reserve. Before he left, he had a meeting with Ta-Tonka Black Bull, chief of the Sioux. They agreed to let them pass through their territories. These tribes are around Moose Jaw. They had several Indian ponies to accompany Whitecap's party and several men to serve as guides.

They took on their sled, a supply of bacon, tea, sugar and tobacco. They also took a tent and stove and a small supply of wood in case they would not find any along the way. It was bitterly cold when they left. They were in territory they did not know, so they were glad they had guides to show them the right trails. The trip took 10 days."

I am surprised how much building has been going on in the winter cold. Sutherland School opened. The Drinkle Block is finished. The CNR freight sheds are being built. I see problems ahead with their location.

We had Hugh's 12th birthday. He got new skates and hockey stick. His old ones will adorn Jim's feet. Both boys are keen to go outside to skate. Hugh was happy there was still some left over baking from Christmas. We also gave him the book "The Story of Champions by Howard Pyle. His special birthday wish was to pass snow shovelling on to Jim – then he wished he had two, so he passed up to Willie his job of bringing wood upstairs.

Willie and Hugh have lots of friends. Sometimes they are with Henry Rose's son. Henry runs auctions on Victoria. Of course, Glen Headly is a staunch friend of both boys. I sometimes wonder about Willie's newest friend, Freddy Badger. His Dad is a wine clerk at the Saskatchewan Hotel. I think Freddy might not be a good influence, but maybe Freddy's mother says the same thing about Willie! While the boys share some friends, Hugh has some gentle friends. He is great friends with Lyle Gustin who is already a gifted pianist. Hugh loves to listen to Lyle practise.

We are slowly finding our way socially. The children attend Sunday School and I sometimes go to the Women's Missionary Society. Rev. Gallop got Arch to join the Royal Temples and Archie enjoys it.

In one of February's papers was an article about horses. Willie is always interested as he still misses our horse we left in Morden. High Way Store on 2nd Avenue and 23rd Street brought in a load of horses. The horses weigh between 1,000 lbs. and 1,800 lbs. They vary in price from $250 to $650.

February 1909

I have finished the list of all our books. At first I was going to record them all here, but the list is too long. We have 80 books.

I seem to be making lists. Using the Henderson Directory, I recorded businesses in Saskatoon. There are 8 churches, 28 blocks, apartments and public buildings, 3 public schools, 2 newspapers, 7 chartered banks, 8 licensed hotels. Some of the businesses are 4 flour mills, a sash & door, a machine shop, many grocery and meat stores, factories. The city has its own gas and electric plant. There is a pumping plant for the water system. So far they have 34 thousand feet of water mains and 29,000 feet of a sewer system. I am glad we have both services and they are expanding rapidly. The sewage is piped to 1 mile below the CPR bridge and enters the river.

March 1909

The Nutana School Board announced it plans to increase the number of classes from 4 to 8. In January they had 12 new pupils enroll and February's total was up to 126 pupils. Attendance and punctuality are ongoing problems, so the Board implemented this plan: the classroom with the highest percentage of attendance for the month will get a half day holiday.

April 1909

This month saw a rush of settlers coming here. Cars from various points are bringing new settlers. CPR reported two cars from Perth and Smith Falls, Ontario. There were two boxcar loads for Sutherland and 4 cars are headed for Wilkie. CNR had 2 cars transferred from Grand Trunk Railway carrying in settlers' effects.

The Saskatoon Piano and Organ Co. had a sale of pianos, organs and sewing machines. We had been thinking of getting a piano, so we thought we would buy one for Nan's birthday. Of course, it will be shared by the family. We chose a $500 Bell piano on sale for $325. We are going to have it delivered closer to her birthday.

Sometimes the newspaper prints pupils' marks. I question why it is called the Honour Roll, as many are not so honourable! Willie's grade VIII listed Willie as 8th out of 11. I am not making excuses for him, but often marks are given for having memorized facts put down. Often the depth of understanding is not tested, and for pupils like Willie, that doesn't seem fair to me.

May 2, 1909

Yesterday was Nan's 9th birthday. She is growing up so quickly. She is more organized than I am. She is doing well in her class and was the top student. Of course, Willie somewhat sarcastically commented she was the ideal student because she could memorize easily and is conforming. Arch replied that we need conformers in the world as well as non-conformers and dreamers. Willie likes to think he is somewhat of a radical thinker, but Arch hastened to add that the world needs both and one type isn't better than another.

Of course, Nan was thrilled with the piano! I play a little and so I can get her started. If she is faithful to practicing for a year, we will let her take proper lessons.

We gave her two of Andrew Lang's Fairy books. I made her a cake to resemble a piano. I cut a 9 x 12 pans in two lengthwise, so the cake was 24" long. The black keys had to be dark brown instead. Piano cakes test my ability to the limit. I could not produce people or animal cakes. She did not choose to pass on her chores but had a great idea. In no time she figured out "Twinkle, Twinkle, Little Star" and "Do You Know the Muffin Man". After we sang those two several times, it was getting a little thin. So, she requested each person to say a nursery rhyme. The older children got into the spirit. I soon realized that Helen and Geordie did not know many. I spent more time singing, telling stories and reading to the older ones. I was not feeling very well for a couple of years after Geordie was born, so that is probably the reason.

At Nan's request, her father started and recited

"Ride a cock horse to Banbury Cross
To see a fine lady upon a white horse.
Rings on her fingers and bells on her toes,
She shall have music wherever she goes."

Geordie's expression was precious. He glanced at my feet (He knows my name is Belle and you could see him imagining time bells – me – on her toes. Also, Arch has given me several nice rings which I wear on special occasions!

Hugh went next. He recited "Wee Willie Winkle in his nightgown". Again, Geordie's expression was priceless, as he imagined his big brother running up and down stairs in a nightgown. Jim followed with "Georgie Porgie, pudding and pie, kissed the girls and made them cry". I recited an old favourite, "Rockabye Baby, on a treetop". Nan just shone as she is rarely the centre of attention. Nothing is sweeter than our family laughing together.

I look forward to having a garden. Arch decided the soil should be richer, so he had topsoil brought in. Willie spaded it in and Hugh and Jim keep raking it. I love growing flowers – onions not so much. I plan to have caragana along the front and down the east side. I want some peonies, bleeding hearts and roses. Also some favourite annuals are bright flowers like cornflowers, sweet peas, bachelor buttons and straw flowers.

Our house is quite close to our neighbours to the west, so we are going to put up a fence together. Arch doesn't have time so Mr. Raul is building it and Willie and Hugh will help. I want a lawn in the front yard and down the east side and under the stationary clothesline.

June 1909

The June 2nd newspaper reported that at least 44 stray dogs have been destroyed. Peter Cameron, the dog catcher, has been taking his job seriously. More strays were in Saskatoon and Riversdale, but even we were affected. There was a fair amount of excitement on our street. Word had been circulated Cameron would be scouring Nutana, so everyone was warned to keep their dogs in the house or at least tied up. The dog catcher was over on Twelfth Street. Coming home from school at noon, the boys noticed McConnell's black Lab running loose across the street. No one was home at McConnell's but luckily Rex answered the boys' calls. They were all breathless and asked if we could keep the do inside our house until after school.

So I found myself caring for Rex. He was very polite, and I enjoyed his company very much. All ended well, but when we read about the dog hunt, everyone thought we had maybe saved a life! Further, the report said 10 dogs without tags were shot Monday evening. They had warned citizens that all dogs need a tag for 50¢. Mr. McConnell told us they had neglected getting a tag because usually Rex was tied up or under supervision. The McConnells sent Clifford across to thank me.!

June 9 - Honour Roll lists were in today's paper. Willie's teacher, Mr. Graham, is the teacher for Grades VIII and VII. He is a very tough marker and so there were no A's. Willie led the class with the highest average. Others receiving B's were Irma Summerfeld and Lulu Schmidt. The B's had a total of 9 names. The rest listed were C's and D's.

July 5, 1909

Willie's birthday was on the 2nd and Jim's was on the 4th. They agreed they were mature enough to share. Willie turned 14 and Jim 11. We gave Willie an old classic, "Black Beauty" since he loves horses. Jim got "Peter Pan" by J.M. Barrie.

Everyone had wanted to buy soda from the Saskatoon Bottle Works, but we just couldn't start buying them for six children. We gave the two boys money to go and pick out 10 bottles, two each for the birthday boys, and one each for the rest of us. Hugh went along to help carry. Each of the boys wanted and English Root Beer and Cream Soda. I was pleased when Hugh suggested we share so we could taste more. Strawberry Soda was the favourite of the youngest three. We are saving the bottles and I can fill them with lemonade. We also gave the boys money to go to the fair in August, with enough money for Hugh as well.

July 20, 1909

The garden is doing well. It is a treat to have fresh lettuce, green onions and radishes.

August 7, 1909

The boys got to the fair. It is at a new location. They had a wonderful time on rides and eating and drinking!

August 13, 1909

Mrs. Cowan, a widow, sold the car she won at Cairns' contest for $1,075. I wish they reported who won the horses!

September 1909

A real milestone for Saskatoon. On September 2, the university officially opens. Although the classes are not yet in a proper university site, classes leading to a B.A. and a B.SC, are being offered, Tuition is $300 a year.

The September 7 newspaper reported a story about Cairns' car mishap. He was driving his fine McLaughlin Buick on a holiday trip. 5 ½ miles this side of Dundurn a heavy traction engine was passing through and the custom was to spread a lot of hay. Mr. Cairns started to drive right over the top of the straw. The pile of hay was pushed ahead and he accelerated to drive over it. At the front end, it caught fire. I think he wished he had the car that Mrs. Cowan sold!

Finally building has started in our block. At the bottom of 400 block, there are two new builds and William Cooper is living in his new house. The next two lots are still empty and then our neighbour, Richard Raul at 418 and then our house.

October 1909

We had Geordie's 5th birthday. Arch was away so we just had cake. His book was "Tale of Ginger and Pickles by Beatrix Potter and a Crokinole board. We had to play endless games of "I spy with my little eye"!

Lots of building permits were taken out this year. This year's totals are $890,667. I notice, by the list, that there were a considerable number on the west side, on Avenues D, E and even H. The houses seem to be around $2,000 to $3,500.

November 1909

A new curling rink is being built between the foot of 4th Avenue and Spadina. This will be temporary until next year. There are 7 sheets covering property of 100' x 200'. They already have a stockpile of valuable lumber worth $1,500. Next year the new rink will be worth $5,000.

Some of the marks for the collegiate for the month of October are in the paper. The top mark was 80 for Ethel Preston. I kept reading down for 28 names and finally found Willie about 15 from the bottom. Arch was not pleased. With an enrolment of 110 pupils, only about 40 of the marks were worthy of publishing on the Honour Roll. It almost embarrassing that Willie even had his name published.

I must be getting old, but I forgot to record Helen's 8th birthday. She loves soup so we only had that with fresh buns. Because Nan had such an expensive gift in May, we bought Helen the most deluxe doll house, which was five dollars. In her mind, the doll house equalled a real piano!

Helen loves school and could read a little before she started. She is so much fun. She loves to curl up in the big chair with Willie who reads out loud to her. The he gets her to read to him. Willie will often make lists of short words and make her sound them out. Willie would make a fine teacher! Helen's book was another of Beatrix Potter's – "The Tale of Jimmy Tiptoes".

A little thought! When I was 17, I was smitten with a young man. My father said I was too young to even consider marriage. As the years rolled by, I was sure I would remain a spinster. Then I met Arch Munro. He was very stable, and serious about marriage. We got married January 19, 1894. Willie was born in 1895, Hugh in 1897, Jim in 1898. Nan was born in 1900. So we had four children in five years. Helen arrived in 1902 and Geordie in 1904! If I had married at 17, I could have had another six or seven children and they would not be as fine as those I do have. Thank you, wise Father!

The Honour Roll marks for Grad VII were also published. The teacher is W.E. Graham. There was only 1 A, Emma Parr, 6 B's and then Hugh was 4th in the C's.

There is a terrible outbreak of Typhoid. This week, 17 were in City Hospital with others turned away. About 90 cases have been cared for at St. Paul's. Even a train conductor on the Goose Lake line says he brought a hundred cases to the city. The mayor of P.A., Mayor Cooke died from typhoid.

I just noticed that I did not record the opening of City Hospital, the first publicly owned hospital in Western Canada. Also, St. Paul's Hospital opened in the former J.H. Willoughby's residence.

December 1909

Saskatoon seems to love contests. This one was sponsored by the Circulation Department of The Phoenix. Miss Louella Patterson won a Bell piano worth $570. Gertrude London won a dining room set worth $150. Mabel Peters won a lady's fur coat worth $100. A point of interest is The Daily Phoenix has a circulation of over 2,000.

The paper said the present population of Saskatoon numbers about 9,000. In 1901, 96 people were listed – and those were adults. There were only two teachers and 113 pupils. The growth figure until the end of 1908 showed there were 16 teachers for 651 pupils. This year will close with 19 teachers and 831 pupils. I wonder if 1910 will surpass these figures by as much.

I will be quite busy for the rest of December. I want to do a lot of baking this year. I am sewing new nightgowns for the girls and night "sacks" for the boys. Arch is starting to look like a round little elf in his night attire!

1910

January 4, 1910

It is a cold Wednesday in Saskatoon and I will not be going out today, but the children reported how they loved the crunchy sound of the snow as they walked home for lunch.

It is hard to believe we have been in Saskatoon for about 18 months. I love our new house. Ours and the house next door have house numbers. The children are all happy at school. The enrolment is growing very rapidly with new pupils every month. The new school opened in May last year was named Victoria. It was already over capacity, so they re-opened the old stone schoolhouse. Willie's class, the older pupils, were kept in the old classroom, while Hugh, Jim and the girls are in the new school. Also in May of 1909, the two School Boards joined. Time will tell if it is a good idea, but personally, I think Nutana should remain Nutana;

leave the Saskatoon Board to pay their separate costs. The enrolments downtown are growing by leaps and bounds and why should Nutana help pay for new schools they need?

While Arch loved his job, sometimes there were problems. Here he is changing a tire.

Arch loves his job travelling for Blue Ribbon Tea. He is gone almost all week. He gets home early on Friday and is home Saturday and Sunday. This little town is growing beyond anyone's imagination. I wonder how it will be in years to come.

Perhaps it is because of the weather, or that January 1 was my mother's 83rd birthday that I am unsettled in my thoughts. Willie, now 14, made an interesting comment the other day. He is a very deep thinker and he said how he needed to express his many thoughts into words. Further, the words then in spoken form cry out to be written down. My thoughts lately have been about my childhood and I feel the need to solidify them by recording them.

My parents, Neil and Helen Stewart, were both born in Scotland in the Perth district. Dad was born in 1828 and my mother in 1827. My mother's maiden name was McKeith. I insisted that Willie's second name be McKeith. They were married in 1851. My sister Maggie arrived 14 months after their marriage and my sister Mary was born 22 months later. My brother, John was born in 1856, so my parents had three children in the space of four years. I beat her record by having my three boys in the space of 3 years, almost to the day!

My father was a well-respected stonemason and was doing very well, but he heard about the opportunities in Canada. He secured a position to help do the stonework on the Parliament Buildings in Ottawa.

They settled around Almonte, 25 miles south of Ottawa.

For whatever reason, my mother had a four year space before my brother Dan's birth in 1862. Going back to her original pattern of two year spacing, my sister Alice was born two years later. I arrived on December 20, 1866. I guess I was supposed to be the family's Christmas present. Two years later they had a baby that lived only six days.

I was the cherished "baby of the family" for four years. My brother William appeared almost 5 years later. I did not like him. Luckily, Alice being two years older and wiser, made him her special project. When I reached the same maturity as Alice, my favourite brother, James Alexander Stewart was born May 12, 1871.

By this time my older sisters were in their late teens. My father worked very hard and provided well for his fairly large family, but the call of the west beckoned him. The Parliament Buildings were finished and also buildings around the Almonte area were done.

Granny Stewart and her five daughters – Margaret, Alice, Isobel, Helen and Mary.

I was just 6 and James a baby when we moved. I don't remember much of the journey, but I do remember riding in a Red River Ox Cart near the end of the trip – destination Winnipeg and area. I made the local newspaper when shortly after I arrived, I went exploring and soon got lost in the tall prairie grasses. The newspaper described how many people searched for me. My bond with my father became even stronger, as he was the one who found me. I was full of scratches and bites, but I do remember his strong arms carrying me home and placing me in the arms of my beloved mother.

Our life was good. We had a lovely home and plenty of food and love.

Although I had not been born in Scotland, I always considered it my birthplace. Our parents told us many stories about the "old country" and mother always sang the traditional Scottish songs and hymns. She loved Burn's songs, such as "Ye Banks and Braes of Bonnie Doon", "Comin' Through the Rye", "John Anderson My Jo" and, of course "Auld Lang Syne". My favourite was this old tune and I think it was my mother's, too.

"O sing to me the auld Scotch sangs, i' the braid
Scottish tongue,
The sangs my father wish'd to hear,
the sangs my mither sung,
When she sat beside my cradle or croon'd
me on her knee,
And I wadna sleep, she sang sae sweet
the auld Scotch sangs to me.
And I wadna sleep, she sang sae sweet
the auld Scotch sangs to me.

Sing ony o' the auld Scotch sangs, the
blithesome or the sad.

They mak' me smile when I am wae,
and greet when I am glad.
My heart goes back to auld Scotland;
the saut tear dims my e'e;
And the Scotch blood leaps in a' my veins,
as ye sing the sangs to me.
And the Scotch blood leaps in a' my veins,
as ye sing the sangs to me."

Enough for now, my thoughts are written down. My restlessness has vanished and I hear wee Geordie Mack awakening from his nap. I start to sing the old Scots tunes and joy springs up again. Yes, it is a cold, cold day in Saskatoon to start the new year, but I am snug and warm, with love of Arch and children dear and I look forward to a wonderful New Year.

I see I did not record anything about Christmas 1909. Our Christmas was uneventful. My mother sent mitts for everyone, including Arch and me, that she had knit. She is remarkable as she turned 83 on January 1st.

Our bookshelves are filling up. Willie got "The Head of Kay's", Hugh's book was "The Adventures in the Panama" by Frank Baum. Jim got Frank Baum's newest book, "The Boy Fortune Hunters in Egypt". We started the girls on the Queen Series by Frances Burnett and

Geordie's book was "The Tale of Sammy Whiskers". Arch surprised me with Harold Bell Wright's new book "The Shepherd of the Hills". We gave Arch another book by Ralph Connor, "Beyond the Marshes".

The family got "Rook" and we played endless games of "Old Maid" and "Snap" with the younger ones.

January 29, 1910

We celebrated Hugh's 13th birthday. He is the only one whose birthday is definitely in the cold of winter (except me, December 20th).

March 15, 1910

I have not written anything in the last month or so. I have not been feeling too well. Arch has pushed me to go to the doctor, but I know what it is. I am 45 years old, and so . . .

I still make supper, but when Arch isn't home, the two boys make breakfast. They have been taking their lunches to school in this cold weather. Jim is so kind – he is always offering to make a spot of tea – just as his father does when he is home. Geordie is good about playing quietly on his own and is not the kind of child who gets into mischief!

Today the John East Foundry opened. Apparently, many spectators observed the first product. While it may be wonderful, I don't like that area of town. Arch's youngest brother P.J. (Peter James) and his wife Pearl had a house built in the 100 block of Avenue B. While the house is similar to ours, even a little bigger, I think location is the most important factor. P.J. is very involved in the wheeling and dealing of the real estate market.

April 1, 1910

We have just made a huge decision. Arch really wants a touring car and I certainly see the advantages.

I had wanted a house with a lovely frond verandah, but there is no room there, so an addition across the back makes sense. I have worked it out in my mind. I want it right across the back and 12" wide. The part where the back door is will have wood up to waist level, then glass on top. I want a shelf around to put plants on. Then a screen door will lead to the left, a summer area. That area will be screened in on the top half with some wooden bottoms and more ledges for plants. I saw this idea in my Good Housekeeping magazine. For the screened in large part, sheets of plywood 9" X 12' will be put over the screens from the insides to protect from winter snow getting in. The panels will be painted white. We definitely need something to protect the kitchen door. Also, the floor in the side leading to the kitchen door will have a place for jackets and hats (spring, summer and fall). On the floor there will be room to line up dusty shoes and muddy rubber boots.

We approached Mr. McConnell across the street who is a contractor. He will build it for $600 and he offered to build a shed shelter, for our proposed car, on the southwest side for $50 if the boys help carry lumber. I told Arch a shelter ready for his new car represents hope for a bright future. R. Connell's crew will start to build the addition. I am sure it will add value to the house. I can already see 20 clay pots on the ledges. Outside, I will plant tall flowers and Arch will make some wire fencing for climbing sweet peas.

The Phoenix published a long list of houses for sale. The prices seem to be between $2,000 and $4,500. Also, lots of apartment buildings are being built, with prices around $35,000 to $40,000.

Before I forget, although not likely, I will record my encounter with Mrs. Diefenbaker. The Diefenbaker family moved into the new bungalow at 411 Ninth Street. They have two boys, John, the older is Willie's age. Elmer is between Jim and Nan. I sent Willie down to welcome john and to invite him to join in with Willie and the neighbourhood boys. Willie came home fairly soon. I tried to question him, but all Willie would say is "something is weird". So, I sent Mrs. D a note to invite her to come to tea at our house. I must say, I was surprised when she appeared, as she is a fellow Scot, not German as I had assumed by the name.

At first, the visit was fine, but soon every topic turned into praise for the wonders of son John. She made it clear that Willie was not on the same intellectual level as her son! She showed no interest in any topic other than John. It was quite rude of her, as she didn't inquire about any of our children. She announced several times that they had only the two boys, and there was no note of regret, but rather seemed a point of pride. I usually don't, but I took a strong dislike to that woman.

I could not hold back a chuckle when the school marks were published. In Elmer's class, there were 4 with an A, 18 with B's and Elmer led the 5 C's. Then John's mark was 62%, Our Hugh usually fits into the C category, and he is not a keen pupil!

May 31, 1910

On May 7, it was reported that King Edward VII died of pneumonia. A diplomat heralded him as a good King and a Friend of Peace. His son, the Prince of Wales, will become King George V. In Saskatoon, two funeral church services were held. The English flocked to St. John's, while many Scots attended Knox Presbyterian. People of other denominations had to choose. More definitely went to St. John's. Most businesses were closed for funeral hours.

On May 25th, the Saskatchewan Musical Association presented a programme in Saskatoon. The city asked for volunteers, with autos, to drive the out-of-town participants from the Flanigan Hotel. I took Nan to an afternoon session. She was inspired by all the performances and has great visions for a musical career playing the piano. I hate to say this, but this will turn out to be a pipe dream, minus the organ.

Arch came home on the weekend with Great News – great, at least, to him! He bought 80 acres about 5 miles out of Marsden. I don't know what to think. It is so far away. He paid $200 for it. It has a modest house, a small barn and an outhouse. Basic furnishings – kitchen table and six chairs, a pump, a kitchen range, a cupboard for dishes, a double bed and a cot used as a sofa. For now, he can rent the land to Alex Rutherford, who has a neighbouring 80 acres. Arch has visions when he retires, we would move there and build a better house. I am not arguing now but will never leave my house here. I have too many lovely things – furniture, good dishes and rugs. If the time comes, I have another card; there is no Presbyterian Church nearby.

The legal description of the lot is NW ¼ Section 18-45-26 West of 3rd.

June 30, 1910

It has taken me a couple of weeks before I could write about this tragedy. Our dear Doctor McKay – how our hearts bleed for him. Although we did not socialize too much in the past, partly because of his terribly busy workload and Arch on the road so much, we still had a warm friendship. When the twins, Margaret and Hartford were born, I paid a visit with gifts. I was over in early May for another visit with Susanna and the twins. They are just so special.

I can see how I am avoiding writing down the harsh words. Susanna is dead. Her clothes caught fire from her gas stove. He was so shocked, so inconsolable, so wounded.

When word came, Arch and I went there immediately. We offered to bring the twins home with us. I think his grief was so raw, he could not even think of the care they needed. We brought them home, Arch carrying Hartford and I carried Margaret. We had Willie along, who waited outside. He carried all the supplies we had gathered up. We had them for three days.

By coincidence, Susanna came from around Gretna – Morden area. My sister Helen is married to Enoch Winkler. He was the first MLA of that district and knew the family. Enoch went into action. He made arrangements for Susanna's sister and her husband to come immediately on the train. He also hired a trained baby nurse to come along. He did it out of high regard for Dr. McKay.

We are still numbed by the death of Susanna McKay and watching the twins go east. We had a lovely thank you note from her family to thank us for looking after the twins. They are doing well and they promised to keep in touch.

July 1910

We had a muted birthday for Willie and Jim. Willie is now 15 and Jim is 12. Their request was for money to go to the Exhibition. Without making a big show, Arch is giving Hugh money so can go, too.

My spirits are lifting a little. Our new verandah/ porch has been built. We plan to do some painting, but already we have put in a couple of old couches and a cot. The boys have been sleeping in there several times. The garage will have to wait a month or so as Mr. McConnell is overwhelmed with work.

Arch always finds projects to keep the boys busy. He ordered precut planks and 2 by 4's to lay a board sidewalk right up the entire length of the garden. Arch always leaves Willie in charge. I think it is a little unfair because if it not completed, nor up to his standards, he always blames Willie. Willie said to me "I can't do anything right to please my Dad." I tried to pass this on to Arch in a kind and gentle way. Arch spoils the girls and Geordie, so, for their own good, I give them little chores to teach them responsibility.

I want to copy the whole of this report on the Travellers' Day Parade. My youngest brother, James Stewart, has been in the city for a couple of years. He is building a nice business of building and contracting. I really like my sister-in-law, Kate. Their daughter Caroline is Nan's age. Carrie is already gifted at the piano. Their son is called Mack, really named McKeith after our mother's maiden name. I also insisted that be Willie's

second name. Already, Mack is a lively 6 year old boy
– much livelier and more mature than wee Geordie.

Back to the report:

> "The parade started at the ballpark between
> 8th and 9th Streets in Nutana. It came down to
> the CNR Depot and then to the Exhibition
> grounds It was a mile long and some floats
> were pulled by horses. There were three bands,
> two of them from out of town. Almost every
> union had a float in the parade. One person,
> a ticket seller at the Exhibition commented
> he was cold (but better than too hot).

> "The judges were Rev. L.H. Wood, Rev. B.W.
> Fullinger and Fred McKinnon, a mere layman
> found himself in the elevated company for
> this day in question. President of the day was
> A.B. Jones.

We cheered when brother Jim's entry came by. Neatly
and clearly printed:

> "Builder and Contractor
> Estimates given cheerfully and on short notice"

The most exciting part was when a certain roly-poly
clown appeared in a striped baggy suit with ruffles

around his collar and wrists. He had a big red nose and arched eyebrows and wore a pointed hat. It was our father and husband, Archie Munro. He is a very active member of the United Commercial Travellers Association. I made his suit!

Travellers' Day Parade – Arch is second from the right in the stripped suit.

All in all, brother Jim's participation and Arch "clowning around" made it a special time for the two families. Kate and I wanted to watch the parade together. Two women and eight children. Nan and Helen had a great time with their cousin Caroline. Geordie and his cousin Mack (short for McKeith) stayed together. It was good for Geordie to play with a boy his own age. Mack is much more lively and full of fun. He is a favourite of mine because he has the twinkly Stewart/McKeith eyes. Geordie's are rather ordinary Munro eyes.

Our garden is growing nicely and already we are having fresh lettuce. Our grass in the front yard survived the winter nicely and makes the front yard look so tidy.

August 1910

They published all the High School marks in Saskatchewan. John Diefenbaker received his 3rd class certificate. I also noticed a daughter of a friend I made in Prine Albert. Lola Winnifred Muzzy also graduated with 3rd class. She is a beautiful girl with striking features and colouring.

The boys got to the Exhibition on August 10th. It was a good year, as A. Barnes brought his "Big Ring Wild Animals". He claimed he had brought a total of 200 animals. There were seals, a jaguar, pumas, leopards, ponies and elephants. The famous Cameron Highland Band played. Also, the Great Heras Family Show with 3 artistes from Europe. Gymnastic acts were popular. For Willie, the highlight was the ball game between Lethbridge and Saskatoon.

September 1910

The new Nutana Collegiate opened on September 3rd with 95 pupils and 5 teachers. We went to the opening and toured the school. It is an impressive structure. The third floor houses University classes until their buildings are ready next year. August saw piles and piles of lumber, stone and steel at the University site. Gravel piles are ready to make cement. A special spur line was built to get materials on site. 12 box cars laden with material have arrived. Meanwhile, Sir William Laurier was in town to lay the cornerstone at the College Building and also a cornerstone at St. Paul's Cathedral.

November 1910

We had Helen's 8th birthday. The girls have been cutting out Kewpie dolls from my Ladies' Home Journal. Jim was using my dressmaker shears for cutting cardboard. Kewpie Kutouts showed up in the Woman's Home Companion Magazine. Just in time for her birthday, we found Dolly and Friends paper dolls. They were so busy cutting and playing that I don't think she even looked at her new book, "The Cozy Lamb", in the Queen series.

December 1910

I sat down with the telephone book and Henderson's Directory. This is my summary of Saskatoon growth. The population is over 12,000. New builds tripled this year and old buildings sold and resold several times. Schools are overcrowded and more sewer and water lines have been laid. I forgot that there had to be wholesale grocers to supply various stores. The three main ones are Campbell & Wilson Ltd., Codville Co. Ltd. And MacDonald & Co. Can you believe we have 16 laundries, 11 hotels, 4 blacksmiths, two livery and feed stables? Bowman Brothers are selling motorcycles. There are many different trades such as carpenters, contractors and five paint and wallpaper stores. Other services are drays, baggage and express (Canadian National Express and Dominion Express). We have about 18 doctors and even and orchestra – Jackson's Orchestra. The amateur Operatic Society presented H.M.S. Pinafore with 25 musicians and a 60 voice choir. It sold out three nights. The Victory Theatre brought in the first "Talkies." Musical and social groups abound!

There are several reports about Rural Life. For example, two **Doukhobors were fined** $5,000 cash for arson. They burned down 18 schools in the Borden/

Radisson area. They were objecting to having to send their children to public schools.

Oh, yes! Mark Twain died!

We will remember 1910 as a year of great growth in our fine city. God is good!

1911

January 1911

Our Christmas has settled into a pattern of comfort and security in our dear house 422. We did not invite Dr McKay as it would be too painful for all of us. He is working far too hard. I think he uses his work as a cover for his loss.

We did invite brother P.J. I just don't relate to Arch's younger brother. Arch and his older brother Rev. Donald grew up as friends and companions. The fact is that the two Munro lads, Donald and Arch, married two Scottish lasses, Alice Stewart and yours truly. Even that turned out as it should. I would not have been a good partner for Donald. His focus is on the Church and serving God. My sister Alice loves the role of minister's wife and cheerfully runs and attends tall the meeting of them women in their congregation. I would be too worldly.

Alice would have despaired with some of Arch's actions. His beliefs are mainly endless Church on Sunday, prayers and Bible reading every morning, Grace before all meals and bedtime prayers. The rest of the day he is busy living. He loves people, friendships, work, family and lots of action.

We saved New Year's Eve for the Donald Munro family. It happened that Donald had been asked to take a special service at Knox here in Saskatoon. The whole family stayed over two nights. Our children are double cousins and get along so well. Their two girls are about ten years older than our two girls, but they are so patient with Nan and Helen, who look up to them so much. Tassie, the oldest was born in 1891 and George in 1894. Helen is our Hugh's age and John Douglas (we call him Jack) was born in 1899. Our two families made the most of every moment together. Alice and I love to cook and together we cooked the dishes that our mother made. The brothers talked and talked. The Munros are never short of words! It is interesting, some of Arch's stories about his times on the road rubbed off on Donald who seemed to lighten up. Donald's spirituality brought Arch back to the importance of our faith.

The five boys slept on the parlour rug. Donald and Alice slept in the boys' room. The two Helens slept in Willie's tiny room, while Tassie and Nan slept in the girls' room.

February 1911

Near the end of January, there was one little report. I can't wait for Arch to come home and explain. Here is the little report:

> "Berlin: Colonel Galdke says Germany has 5,200,000 trained soldiers and sailors."

Why is that making the news in Saskatoon?

The growth of Saskatoon continues! January papers were filled with reports of development. Even so, building has slowed down a little this winter. But I can't believe how the prices of lots have increased. A 60' lot near Victoria sold for $3,200 and a smaller lot on Main went for $1,800. Properties on 8th Street are packed in 100' lots at $27 per foot! A "dream" home on Main, 7 rooms, full basement, furnace and fireplace was listed at $4,200. Growth on the west side is taking off. Development opportunities between Avenue C and Avenue E are being snapped up. B.A. Archibald sold $30,000 worth of lots there.

I don't understand why this is happening. The old hotel in Nutana has been sold (twice). Mr. Lund bought it from 3 men from Asquith and then sold it to McCann Bros. of Asquith for $40,000.

St. Thomas Presbyterian Church is to build a more suitable building. P.J. and Pearl Munro are members.

The Phoenix reported that Saskatoon's population will be 100,000 in six years. So far, the Saskatoon Club on 21ˢᵗ Street is worth $15,000 and has 190 members.

March 1911

This is the first time Geordie's name is in the newspaper. With perfect attendance, George Munro ranked third out of twenty in the Junior I class.

April 1911

Big plans for a City Hall, the Y.M.C.A. and the King George hotel have been announced. Building permits are being granted for spring builds.

It is reported that regular trains are bringing in newcomers by the thousands. Many will spread out over the province. They say 170 new towns will be born this year in western Canada. Arch cheered and said, "Yay! More people to buy Blue Ribbon Baking Powder!"

Speaking of Blue Ribbon – I pride myself that I do not hide anything from Arch and that we both speak the truth. I am ashamed to say that I prefer Magic Baking Powder over Blue Ribbon. So for about 4 years I have been emptying my Blue Ribbon tin and then filling it with Magic. I felt guilty every time I did it. A while ago Nan caught me doing it. I told her to never let Helen or Jim know or they would squeal on me. Nan promised.

On the topic of baking powder, I have a Blue Ribbon cookbook. Arch thinks it is the housewife's "Bible". I get two women's magazines and they feature new recipes. The cookbook has a special spot in the Hoosier and the magazines are not visible. Arch's idea of praise is "What good baking powder biscuits you made! Yes, Blue Ribbon makes a difference."

Well, I knew Jim and Helen knew my secret when they asked, "Where did you get this delicious recipe?" I never had to actually lie, as Arch would chirp "Blue Ribbon cookbook, of course!" Then they would try to hide their merriment, while I squirmed! The trouble I have discovered about a lie is that each time it is spoken or inferred, guilt increases. But as time goes on, confession does not seem the right thing.

I. F. Cairns has done a lot for Saskatoon growth and development and he built his great store. However, 15 drivers at the store went on strike. It was not against Cairns himself, but they hated the new foreman, so they just put horses and wagons in the stables. Cairns just replaced the drivers. I first thought that was terrible of Cairns, but Arch pointed out he thought Cairns did the right thing. After all, he owns the company and if workers try to change management decisions, chaos will happen. They should have calmly taken their dissatisfaction to Cairns.

May 1911

May 1, St. George's Day, was special for Hugh. He joined the Boy Scouts. He thrives on the discipline and fun of the group. There was a parade and 2 Patrols of the 1st Troop, Saskatoon paraded and then saluted the flag in unison. Even that had to be practised to be in unison. Scoutmaster Johnston is the right kind of leader.

What a great and exciting day was May 19! "Bob" St. Henry, who calls himself "The Bird Man", flew his bi-plane in the city. About 1,000 paid to enter the fairgrounds, but the three boys were some of the many who stayed outside of the gates, so didn't pay.

Air flight is unusual, as they can't control who sees the performance. If you want to see a horse or a circus, one has to pay to see it.

The marks are published again! In Form IIB, Merle Johnston had the top mark of 75. Willie tied with Ruth Mooreman and Clifford Timmons got 62. Seven were lower.

I am a little surprised at my feeling of smugness. John Diefenbaker got only 56! He was right in the middle of his class with 15 pupils with higher marks and 17 lower than his 56. I call that average! I don't think Mrs. D. or myself can brag we have genius sons, but I think Willie is more balanced and is an all-round typical boy. I should show some charity to John, as he has Mrs. D. as a cross – whoops – I meant to say mother.

Cliff McConnell from across the street had a 52. George in Junior I, Room II was 11th out of 21. He likes his teacher, Miss Weir.

May has been a very busy month. David Webster submitted his plans for new Victoria School. It is similar to Caswell with 10 classrooms with cloakrooms. Also, it will have showers and plunge baths. The coronation of George V and Queen Mary took place. Concrete pilings are in for King George Hotel. 130 men are on the building site. They ordered 8 large arc lights so they can add a night shift. The new Queen's Hotel cost $200 thousand and is X5 stories high. It is located on 1st Avenue at 20th Street.

More and more big investors from the East or England or the States are speculating and investing in the city. Millionaires were passing through to the west. They bought a 130' piece of property on the NW corner of 3rd Avenue and 23rd Street for $500 per foot! In other words, $650 thousand. I personally think "too much, too fast".

There is a lot of local money being spent. I.F. Cairns is building a new store on 2nd Avenue and 23rd Street for $275,000, but he works hard at a new project and invests money back into the city.

We (Arch) finally chose our new car. We chose a Maxwell costing $900 delivered, and it is proving very reliable. We only really get to ride in it on Sundays to go to church and sometime a tour around the city.

June 1911

The June 24th newspaper held a special report that Arch drools over. The Automobile Club has announced the rules for July 1 races. The first race on Saturday, July 1st at 7 pm vehicles with 20 hp. On Monday evening, the race for 30 hp machines is for club members only.

Also, Monday evening is the novelty race. Over a five mile course, contestants stop every ½ mile to exchange passengers. Arch plans to join and be ready to win next year! Auto races are planned for runs to Pike Lake and even Watrous.

By the end of summer, several large homes will be completed. Most are located on 15th Street for University Professors. Prof. Rutherford has a Tudor style. Also, a large house has been built for Prof. Bracken. The Petit house on University Drive is beyond imagination. Its cost is $15,000 on a 57' x 50' lot.

Back to 422. Our garden is bountiful. My flowers are doing well. It is so nice to pick fresh vegetables. Hollyhocks are thriving. The children are allowed to pick a carrot whenever they want. They are all careful to pick the larger ones, to give more room for the small ones. Some people plant a lot of potatoes, but since our plot is smaller, we chose to plant just enough for summer use. Sacks of potatoes can be bought in the fall for reasonable prices.

July 1911

The boys again used their birthday money to go to the exhibition. They love the rides and the exhibits. I did take the girls one afternoon to see all the exhibits.

There were prizes for home cooking, handiwork and flowers. We just walked around the rides. Nan and I were content to just watch, but Helen is determined she will next year with her brothers!

There is building taking place on our street. On the north side, the William Murphys are at 409. Diefenbakers are at 411, while Walter Lang lives at 413. And of course, the John McConnells live at 427 across the street. Mrs. Agnes Murray now lives next door where Ernest Dicker lived. On our south side, Mrs. Findlay lives at 410, with the Chambers family at 412. There is still not a house on the empty lot on the other side. I am glad, as the children play there a lot.

September 1911

The school population shot up to 1,478 – about 400 pupils more than a year ago. To match, there are 10 more teachers. The latest census showed our population is around 18,000. It was around 7,000 when we moved her in 1908.

This month, Mr. Alfred Smith, age 75, died. He came here 32 years ago. He was working on the first railroad that was built. For years he worked faithfully for the CPR. He lived over on McPherson and he had a fine garden. His yard won many prizes at the Fair each year. In Henderson's Directory, he was listed as Horticulturist. He motivated others to improve their lots with gardens and flowers. This makes me appreciate how pretty our city is becoming.

September 30. This year I have noticed a difference in me. I have always been so focused on the children and their needs. I realized I was getting almost reclusive. When we go to church, Arch does all the greeting and talking. I had been invited to join women's groups at Knox, but I always found an excuse not to. I started to go with Mrs. Porteous and quite like it. I tend to not go to other places on my own when Arch is away. Believe it or not, I have ventured out to a matinée show. I like going to the Kevin Theatre. They show 5 or 6 short films and in between, they have illustrated songs and the audience sings along. The feature a lot of the popular songs. My favourites are "Put on Your Old Grey Bonnett", "In the Good Old Summertime", and "I've Got Rings on My Fingers". I must admit, I never thought I would be sitting in a public space, singing a son such as "I Wonder Who's Kissing Her Now"! Even some new hymns are getting popular. While I love the traditional ones, I like to hear "The Lower Lights are Burning" and "When the Roll is Called Up Yonder".

October 1911

Jim, past 13 years, has the teacher that both Hugh and Willie had in that grade. This teacher's special thing is to have each pupil choose, memorize and recite a poem. He frowns on poems that are too short or silly. The chosen poem should be very old and tested with time, or it shous teach some virtue, like love or hope or be inspiring. He added a new category – a poem that highlights a way of life. As an example, ethnic differences.

We were discussing this at supper one night and Willie and Hugh said what poems they recited. They could still recite them. Then Helen asked what poems Arch and I learned in school. I told them how memorization was important when we were young. Arch said that we should have a poetry night in three weeks. Nan offered to help Geordie pick a poem and memorize it. Jim insisted that he be last on the programme and reveal his stunning recitation.

The great poetry night was upon us. Arch started with a flourish and dedicated it to me.

A Red, Red Rose

O my Luve is like a red, red rose
That's newly sprung in June;

O my Luve is like the melody
That's sweetly played in tune.

So fair art thou, my bonnie lass,
So deep in luve am I;
And I will luve thee still, my dear,
Till a' the seas gang dry.

Till a' the seas gang dry, my dear,
And the rocks melt wi' the sun;
I will love thee still, my dear,
While the sands o' life shall run.

And fare thee weel, my only luve!
And fare thee weel awhile!
And I will come again, my luve,
Though it were ten thousand mile.

Burns

Willie recited the poem he had prepared three years ago.

All The World's A Stage

All the world's a stage,
And all the men and women merely players;
They have their exits and their entrances;
And one man in his time plays many parts,

His acts being seven ages. At first the infant,
Mewling and puking in the nurse's arms;
And then the whining school-boy, with his satchel
And shining morning face, creeping like snail
Unwillingly to school. And then the lover,
Sighing like furnace, with a woeful ballad
Made to his mistress' eyebrow. Then a soldier,
Full of strange oaths, and bearded like the pard,
Jealous in honour, sudden and quick in quarrel,
Seeking the bubble reputation
Even in the cannon's mouth. And then the justice,
In fair round belly with good capon lin'd,
With eyes severe and beard of formal cut,
Full of wise saws and modern instances;
And so he plays his part. The sixth age shifts
Into the lean and slipper'd pantaloon,
With spectacles on nose and pouch on side;
His youthful hose, well sav'd, a world too wide
For his shrunk shank; and his big manly voice,
Turning again toward childish treble, pipes
And whistles in his sound. Last scene of all,
That ends this strange eventful history,
Is second childishness and mere oblivion;
Sans teeth, sans eyes, sans taste, sans everything.

Shakespeare "As You Like It"

I went next and recited two poems by my favourite Henry Ban Dyke.

If All the Skies

If all the skies were sunshine,
Our faces would be fain
To feel once more upon them
The cooling splash of rain.

If all the world were music,
Our hearts would often long
For one sweet strain of silence,
To break the endless song.

If life were always merry,
Our souls would seek relief,
And rest from weary laughter
In the quiet arms of grief.

One World

The worlds in which we live are two
The world "I am", another world "I do".
The worlds in which we live at heart are one,
The world "I am", the fruit of "I have done".
And underneath these worlds of flower and fruit,
The world "I love" – the only living root.

I don't' think anyone was impressed. The applause was very short and somehow was without heart. Then Hugh recited his favourite.

Ahou Ben Adhem

Abou Ben Adhem (may his tribe increase!)
Awoke one night from a deep dream of peace,
And saw, within the moonlight in his room,
Making it rich, and like a lily in bloom,
An angel writing in a book of gold: —
Exceeding peace had made Ben Adhem bold,
And to the presence in the room he said,
"What writest thou?"—The vision raised its head,
And with a look made of all sweet accord,
Answered, "The names of those who love the Lord."
"And is mine one?" said Abou. "Nay, not so,"
Replied the angel. Abou spoke more low,
But cheerly still; and said, "I pray thee, then,
Write me as one that loves his fellow men."

The angel wrote, and vanished. The next night
It came again with a great wakening light,
And showed the names whom love of God had blest,
And lo! Ben Adhem's name led all the rest.

Leigh Hunt (1784 – 1859)

Geordie wanted to go next. Nan was a great help to him and he did a stellar job of "When I Was Sick and Lay A-bed" by Robert Louis Stevenson. The applause was thunderous and prolonged. Certainly more than mine and so well deserved!

The Land of Counterpane

When I was sick and lay a-bed,
I had two pillows at my head,
And all my toys beside me lay,
To keep me happy all the day.

And sometimes for an hour or so
I watched my leaden soldiers go,
With different uniforms and drills,
Among the bed-clothes, through the hills;

And sometimes sent my ships in fleets
All up and down among the sheets;
Or brought my trees and houses out,
And planted cities all about.

I was the giant great and still
That sits upon the pillow-hill,
And sees before him, dale and plain,
The pleasant land of counterpane.

Nan did a beautiful recitation.

Hope Is the Thing With Feathers

Hope is the thing with feathers
That perches in the soul,
And sings the tune without the words,
And never stops at all,

And sweetest in the gale is heard;
And sore must be the storm
That could abash the little bird
That kept so many warm.

I've heard it in the chillest land,
And on the strangest sea;
Yet, never, in extremity,
It asked a crumb of me.

Emily Dickenson (1830 – 1886)

Helen seemed very nervous. She kept her eyes cast down, almost under the table. She started to do "A Vagabond Song" by Bliss Carman. "There is something in the autumn that is native to my blood." There was a long pause and then Willie shouted out "She is cheating! She has a copy under the table!" Helen never missed a beat. She put the poem on the table exclaiming she did not like that poem. Then she announced her favourite by far – and launched.

Higgledy, Piggledy
My black hen,
She lays eggs for gentlemen.
Sometimes nine,
Sometimes ten,
Higgledy, Piggledy
My black hen.

Even Geordie caught on and said, "That was a nursery rhyme you learned when you were three!" Helen, Helen. She is so much fun, but I worry about her carefree spirit when she is older!

The poem Helen did not prepare for properly:

A Vagabond Song

There is something in the autumn that is
native to my blood—
Touch of manner, hint of mood;
And my heart is like a rhyme,
With the yellow and the purple and the
crimson keeping time.

The scarlet of the maples can shake me like
a cry
Of bugles going by.
And my lonely spirit thrills

To see the frosty asters like a smoke upon
the hills.
There is something in October sets the
gypsy blood astir;
We must rise and follow her,
When from every hill of flame
She calls and calls each vagabond by name.

Bliss Carman (1861 – 1929)

Finally, Jim was ready. He disappeared and came
back wearing a red sash and a hat. He announced that
his poem fit the category "a way of life".

Little Bateese

You bad leetle boy, not moche you care
How busy you 're kipin' your poor gran'pere
Tryin' to stop you ev'ry day
Chasin' de hen aroun' de hay-
W'y don't you geev' dem a chance to lay?
Leetle Bateese!

Off on de fiel' you foller de plough
Den w'en you 're tire you scare the cow
Sickin' de dog till dey jomp the wall
So de milk ain't good for not'ing at all-

An' you 're only five an' a half dis fall,
Leetle Bateese!

William Henry Drummond (1854 – 1907)

Five more verses! He seemed to go on and on! About midway, Arch fled to the kitchen. Worried about him, I went to the kitchen. He was by the back door, trembling, with his hands to his mouth. He choked and said Jim sounded like a Scot who had too much rye! I reminded him that Metis had some Scottish blood in their veins, too.

With a flourish, Jim finished and bowed, with all applauding!

November 1911

There always seems to be a new store opening while another is closing. I am always on the lookout for fabric to make Arch a clown suit. One store advertised they were closing and selling fabric at very low prices. A couple of bolts of black and white striped flannel caught my eye. The cloth had obviously been in the store for a long while, as ends and edges were quite dirty. I thought I might buy enough for a clown suit, but suddenly I had a great idea. I would make all the males sleeping attire to look like jail suits! I bought a Butterick pattern and if the fabric was 27" wide, it would take about 4 yards per person. They had marked it down from regular 30¢ a yard to 10¢ a yard. The clerk must have read my mind, as I am not too good at dickering. He said, "There are over 30 yards here – if you take it all, you can have it for $2.00."

I struggled home with my great purchase. I decided I would make Arch a longer nightshirt and four boys, pajamas. The tops have no collars to fuss with and no plackets nor buttons. The pattern showed a top that was loose and looked more like a baseball shirt. The bottoms are baggy and have a drawstring at the waist to hold them up. Also, the pattern could be made with or without a fly opening. That would take extra time and fabric, so I went with no fly.

I hid the fabric under my bed and tried not to leave any scraps in Willie's bedroom/my sewing room. I am giving them all their attire for Christmas gifts. Usually people see spots before their eyes, but I see black and white stripes after an afternoon of sewing!

I also want to make the girls and myself matching nightdresses. Definitely not stripes or dots!

I took time to make Helen's 9th birthday special. She wanted new boots, so that excursion was a fun day. We had her favourite supper – stew with winter vegetables from our garden. She saw the recipe and picture in my magazine for a Lady Baltimore cake. It was a hit! We played Charades after supper.

December 1911

Usually I make a full report after Christmas, but I found some facts about Canada that I find interesting.

In 1901, Canada had a population of 5,332,150. In 1911, Canada has an estimated population of 7,008,867. In 1901, the only province that had over 1 million people was Ontario. This year, Quebec joined the million dollar club with a population of 1.5 million. Saskatchewan grew from 91 thousand to 153 thousand. As Arch would say, "Yeh! More Blue Ribbon sold!"

It has been a different kind of year. The three older boys are often away with friends. Willie loves playing lacrosse and baseball. When he is home, he is reading. Hugh is growing up, although not so much in size. However, he is very comfortable within. He loves his Boy Scout troop and loves skating. The two boys still do some things together, but they have different circles of friends.

Jim is the lively one! He has a paper route and loves having his own money. He is the most talkative of all the children and always has a smile on his face. I think he will do well in life as he is positive about everything. He genuinely loves everyone. Of the boys, I think he is most like Arch in his approach to life.

Nan has grown a lot this year and is very responsible for an eleven year old. I am glad for her that she was not the first born, as she would have taken on all the responsibility of all the younger ones. Now she cares for Helen and Geordie. She is not a bossy person and both Helen and Geordie respond to her caring ways. Helen is the most like Jim. They both have a sparkle and a sharp wit. Theirs is positive. Willie also has that quality but his can be a little negative or sarcastic at times.

Geordie Mack! He will always be the baby no matter how old he gets. I think he is closest to me and the girls. He has always been an "easy" child to raise.

The Christmas plans are that our family will take the train to North Battleford. We will go on the 23rd of December and come home the 26th. I would love to be there for Hogmanay, but it is too long to leave the house. The Mconnell boys are to come by in the evenings and bank the furnace. In the mornings they will check again. We have to keep the water pipes from freezing.

Everyone is very excited and Arch and I are looking forward to the services at Donald's church.

1912

January 1912

The trip to North Battleford revived my spirits. I had not been away from Saskatoon for over three years. Arch noticed the difference in me and promised he would try to alter his schedule so that he could get home more evenings. He was upset that he had put too much responsibility on me – and on Willie. He even has plans for us to have a summer holiday at Meota.

Alice and Donald went out of their way to make Christmas so special for all of us. George took all the boys out sledding. There is a fine hill nearby. Of course, our girls followed Helen and Tassie everywhere. Helen and Tassie fussed over the girls' hair and even had some special cream that they rubbed on their hands and faces. Tassie is a young adult. She hopes to become a nurse. She is very good at the organ and piano and is the organist at church. She let Nan try the organ and encouraged her to practise more. Helen is so sweet. She is almost 16 and already a very good fancy ice skater. Her disposition is much like our Helen, bubbly and carefree. George is a year older than Willie and is an excellent student.

Alice is a better cook than I am, although she says not. I think her cooking tastes more like our dear mother's.

Alice and Tassie are very good artists. They had painted each of us a little drawing. I am going to put them in frames when we get home. Donald and Alice gave our family a huge book of Bible stories. We gave Alice and their two girls pretty necklaces. We laughed when Alice and I exchanged parcels. There were two shawls, almost identical. The men exchanged bottles of brandy – "for medicinal purposes only".

The biggest excitement were the pajamas. I had enough flannel to make Jack and George matching black and white striped pajamas. I think Donald was a little disappointed but I just couldn't put a man of the cloth and preacher of the Gospel in a jail suit. Besides, I had run out of fabric. The boys all slept on the dining room floor and they announced they were sleepy and had to go to jail. Arch gave me another lovely brooch and a voucher to have a stylish costume made by a professional dressmaker. That certainly brought me out of my depression.

I don't think Arch meant it as a criticism of me, but I took it that way! Meaning to compliment their children, he asked Donald the secret to having such accomplished children. Donald said plain and simple that children must have discipline and they made them practise. Arch, almost apologizing for our children, replied that he was away a lot and that I was not strict enough!

George Munro – Arch's father. Born 1819. Died 1985.

Donald and Archie's father, George Munro, was a very upright man. He was also very nice but had control of all his children. My father, Neil Stewart, was a kind, easy-going person and really spoiled his six daughters. His position was that each person had to choose for themselves and learn self-control – not to be controlled by others. Arch is probably right that I coddle the children, but I first of all want them to be happy children.

Mayor Clinkskill is still our mayor for this year.

The Church put on a Robbie Burns supper. I wore my Stewart tartan sash with my black skirt and fancy white blouse. Arch was asked to "Address the Haggis". He did a splendid job and rolled every "r" and threw in a little Gaelic. I almost burst out laughing when I though he sounded a wee bit like Jim doing "Little Batiste". He had to have a kilt and he does no own one. Mr. McLeod had one and insisted that Arch wear it. His mother was a McLeod. It was near Hugh's 14th birthday, so we took him with us. Now he wants a kilt. They served the traditional Scottish supper. We sang Burns songs and were entertained by pipers and dancers. (The sword dance was Hugh's favourite.)

Brother P. J. is immersed in the Real Estate market. His present firm is Munro, McLean Co. Everyone wants in the market. I have observed that many local companies are investing in land for residential, small apartments and small businesses. The men who were here early, like the Clinkskills, Caswells, Drinkle and Cairns are doing very well, but they are paying unheard of prices for lots. I admire them as they seem to have the welfare of the city as one of their top priorities. They take active roles in civic affairs.

A new trend developing is that out of city or even out of country investors, who have lots of money, are swooping in and making huge profits, but they have no qualms about buying an important piece of land and then quickly selling it, of course, for a handsome profit.

I am using the last newspapers of 1911 to sum up the year. In 1911, King Edward school site was originally bought for $700 and is appraised for more than $110 thousand. Already there are plans for a new King Edward school. The Caswell site that was purchased for $7,000 is appraised at $110 thousand. Also, the new Victoria school and the firehall were built. It is hard to believe that there are over 1,777 pupils with 51 teachers. We have seven schools now – King Edward, Alexandra, Princess, Victoria, Sutherland, Caswell and King George. The reported value of occupied school sites is $354,000 and of unoccupied school sites, $134,000.

February 2, 1912

There was an interesting display when the new fire truck, drawn by three horses, was tested. They tested the new ladder system at the King George Hotel to reach the top windows. The ladder on the truck is in two sections. To raise it, a small wheel is turned to release a spring. This brings the first section to the desired elevation. Then a second crank is used to run up the second section. There is a great need for equipment that can reach higher floors.

It was reported that 720 lots sold in one day in the Buena Vista area. They are the last of an 80 acre area, with only 9 lots left.

March 30, 1912

George McCraney, M. P. raised the idea to start a Forestry Farm. The Dominion Government bought a ½ section north of Sutherland for $20,000. I think that will prove to be a very good investment.

Yesterday the "Kipling C. N. R. car crashed through the bridge and fell fifty feet to the ice. 13 people were injured.

April 1912

I thought 1911 was a blur of land and building exchanges, but already this year the new $150,000 Barry Hotel opened. Tenders have been called for Westmount School. The building permits for April totalled $1,431,600. It seems now that builders and contractors will build several houses in a row, basically all the same. I am glad that our house is not like others on the street.

On a different topic, on April 14, Titanic sank with 1.517 lost souls. Only 700 survived. What a tragedy!

Here we go again, Dr. McKay! He condemned 40 thousand lbs. of food. Watermelons from Alabama took 15 days in transit and were not stored in a cool place. Can you imagine 28,600 lbs. of stinking watermelons? 5,000 lbs. of flour were contaminated as well as 6,000 lbs. of various groceries. There were 1,100 lbs. of pork and another 627 lbs. of various meats also contaminated. In my eyes, Dr. McKay is a hero and a shaper of the city.

May 28, 1912

The garden is in. I am glad the boys do most of the work. I could spend all day tending flowers.

The girls' latest rage is hopscotch. I found a recipe to make their chalk. Mis a cup of Plaster of Paris with ¾ cup of water and mix well. I add a quarter cup of paint for colour. Pour into moulds. The girls do a lot of skipping, also.

I notice a lot of the boys in the neighbourhood are obsessed with playing marbles. Although Willie and Hugh say they are too old to play, if no one is around, they challenge Jim to a game. They usually win and Jim starts to howl. He doesn't notice them returning his marbles to his bag later.

To further highlight my statement about "outside" investors, the President of the Saskatoon Auto Club asked for volunteers with cars to pick up 67 men and 5 women from British manufacturers interested in investing her. The city will host a lunch and then the cars will take them on a tour. More than 70 auto manufacturers are using self-starters. More women will be driving as it was too hard for them to crank.

The newspapers are just full of sales, deals and building. For example, the Hotel Saskatchewan in Regina on Main and Saskatchewan, that was bought for $38,000 sold for $100,000. Another example of speculating – a company in Winnipeg bought 500 lots in River Heights for $125,000. Just watch – soon those lots bought for approximately $250 each will be resold separately for much more!

I must stop following all this! I must remind myself that life is more than about money. Values such as stable families and love are far more important. (However, I must admit that I am fascinated with these activities. I sometimes wish I had been born a male, with lots of money to play with!)

June 15, 1912

On a lighter note, J. P. Murphy of the city drove from Los Angeles to Portland, Oregon. He left Portland on May 27th and arrived in Saskatoon on June 10th. He scorned a few offers to have horses tow the car through mud.

July 2, 1912

On June 30th, Regina was hit by a cyclone. Twenty-eight people were killed and about 300 injured. About 2,500 are homeless and 500 business are destroyed. At the Legislature, all exam papers for Saskatchewan grade schools were sucked out of the building. The cyclone lasted 6 minutes.

Bill (Willie) and Nan in 1912.

Today is Willie's 17th birthday. He has a job to do for a neighbour, so we are going to wait and celebrate on the 4th with Jim's 14th birthday. At Jim's suggestion, we will walk to the park and have a picnic supper.

July 3, 1912

What a week. Yesterday there was a huge fire at J. F. Cairns' store. Today he already has 150 men to move away debris and carpenters are starting on the roof.

July 4, 1912

It is evening and the double birthday was a success. Both birthday boys had their favourite foods, and each had a decorated cake bought at the baker. I felt guilty as I decided not to make them myself, but cyclones, fires and hot days dampened my enthusiasm for baking. The three boys said they wanted to do something special. The did not reveal their plan until supper, so it was hard to say "no". They are off to the new Daylight Theatre at night. The theatre is enormous, with 980 seats. The attraction is that they have the longest film programme. They feature 8 reels; each reel is 12 – 15 minutes long. The boys are anxious to see the reel about a man-eating tiger. They will be home late, so I am going to bed, but doubt I will sleep until I hear them come in. My three boys are all in their teens, so we have to let them go.

July 13, 1912

The new Knox Church should be ready in May next year. We have been going to Westminster for a couple of years. We are not going to join the new congregation. I shouldn't say it, but the planning committee are the University and wealthy types. It is being designed in

Montreal, will cost $129,000, exclusive of the organ, seats and three huge stained glass windows. The simplicity of the old Kirk is forgotten, and to me, it will seem more like a concert hall than a simple church.

August 15, 1912

The Exhibition and parade were great successes. I had made Arch a new clown suit. I have a good basic pattern that is right for him. This year the prime colour is royal blue. Then in yellow, I cut out suns and stars and hand stitched them. There were 9 bands in the parade. Then Sales and Flote Circus featured at this year's Ex, added elephants and camels. One section of the parade had native costumes of all climes. The biggest ethnic costume section was the Sons of Scotland. This walking group followed the Pipe Band. I think every kilt in the city was marshalled to "walk" in the parade. A sizeable group of Indians also made a fine display.

September 1912

The Henderson's Directory put out their fifth edition. There are about 31,000 listings, almost double last year's edition.

A contract to supply the furnishings for the Y. M. C. A. was given to J. F. Cairns. Their prices were lower than the Hudson's Bay Company or the T. Eaton Company and of better quality (so says Mr. Cairns).

Another long time investor and builder in the city sold his holdings to an English Syndicate for $750,000.

September 30, 1912

Saskatoon loves its contests! Now it is the "Book Lore Contest". This one is huge, but to me, complicated! The paper published a series of picture, each representing the title of a book. They provided a coupon, with a place for title and author, plus information for the person who entered. Ther were 530 pictures. Prizes ranged from a player piano worth $750, won by Mrs. Hackoin of Souris. She had 60 correct. Then prizes descended down to a 114 piece set of Limoge dinnerware, worth $210. That was won by Mr. Nicholson of Whitewood. Third prize was a Victor Victrola, worth $210. Very rapidly, prizes were worth less and less. Winners 11 – 15 won a box of 110 cigars. Then a lot of books were prizes. Winners 50 – 149 also won cigars. Winners 150 – 250 won boxes of Fry's chocolates, worth $1 each and finally, winners 2501 – 351 won a picture of King George and Queen Mary.

I started to enter, but lost interest because there were so many pictures and many of them of books I had not even known. Even so, my entries won me a picture of the King and Queen.

I don't think they will ever have this contest again as it was too large and too complicated. If the top person managed only 60 correct answers out of so many, it was too difficult.

October 15, 1912

At the beginning of October, Porter's Freak Animal Show was in town. It was touring from Atlantic to Pacific. They had 40 animals that were freaks of nature. Again, the three boys wanted to go. Arch was out on the road, so I gave my permission. Arch was very upset when the boys started to describe what they saw and was somewhat cross with me. Willie, particularly, is very headstrong and Arch doesn't realize how difficult it is for me to make decisions. These are some of the freak animals they saw: a bull with a bulldog's head and face, a Jersey cow with 5 legs, another Jersey cow with 2 sets if udders, one extending from the back.

There was a steer with its heart on the left side of the neck. I agree with Arch that this does not belong at the supper table.

I just read in the newspaper that Saskatoon has the record number of autos per capita in North America. In fact, 100 car loads of cars will arrive next spring. Too bad they don't run on Blue Ribbon baking powder!

On Geordie's birthday, the 3 boys took him to see a baseball game and, of course he received a new ball glove.

All fall, building is going on in Nutana. Innes is to build a 3 storey building on the southwest corner of Victoria and Main. Hartley Chube is to build an apartment on Main. A new subdivision from University straight south is being created. It is called Broadway Addition and adjoins Buena Vista. Also, the cornerstone was laid for the new $120,000 school in Sutherland. The one I was impressed with, and Arch took us in the car to see, are the two sets of lovely iron gates at the Forestry Farm.

I cannot believe the population of Saskatoon is listed at 27,529 thousand. Predictions are, that by 1917, the population may be up to 100,000.

The paper reported that there are 101,536 Indians in Canada and 4,600 Eskimos. To help Indians to progress, there are 325 Residential Schools. I think the government is really trying their best.

The biggest news in the city so far is the master plan to build a whole new city. A gigantic American Syndicate has bought 475 acres across from the Silverwoods. They are calling it Henley Park. What a climax for the year with great promise that next year will be a banner one in the growth of the city.

The D. D. Campbell Real Estate Company claims they sold 80 lots in a few minutes. I think they are stretching their figures as how is that even possible?

There have been advertisements in the paper almost every day. The writer certain is verbose. For example:

"Twixt the Optimist and the Pessimist,
The difference is droll.
The Optimist sees the doughnut,
The Pessimist, the hole."

I wonder where they stole that!

Also, in October 1912, Dr. John McKay reported 135 cases of typhoid. 100 cases were at City Hospital and 35 cases at St. Paul's. There were 6 deaths. When will people ever listen and learn? He has laboured for five years to keep citizens safe. Forget the fancy buildings and sidewalks. He tackled the butchers and slaughterhouses and was verbally attacked. He was so vocal, he was made Medical Health Officer. He tackled the typhoid cause, pinpointing contaminated water and mild supplies. Many grocery stores and restaurants fought against him actually going into their basements where he found horrible storage problems. He hired a microbiologist to identify bacteria. He encouraged a healthy lifestyle. He was instrumental in getting a swimming pool and a riverbank hill for winter activities. I would never have thought to, but he examined how horses and wagons collecting night soil from the privies create a problem. He went after private wells and slaughterhouses. He used education or sarcasm to help people follow the health regulations.

December 1912

We had a wonderful little supper for Helen's 10th birthday. I made her favourite desert – apple pie – and the weather is cold enough to keep ice cream frozen, so that went well with the pie. We had planned that we would play Charades and then poop some corn, but at the supper table, Hugh started it by teasing Helen with a memory of her. When Helen was six, they had races at the Sunday School picnic. Helen sped to the finish line, leaving all others behind her. She was so excited as she knew she would get a ribbon. When they presented her with a red ribbon, she looked shocked and upset. We asked what was bothering her. She replied that she thought she would get to pick, and she wanted to win a "blue ribbon" to please her father. (Sometimes, I think The Blue Ribbon Company is made too much of by Arch.)

That led to Willie telling how he remembers how, when Helen was about one or two years old. If she didn't get her way, she would not cry, but her dear little mouth turned down into a pout. Her lip would tremble, and a tear would trickle down her cheek. Then if she got her way, or a toy she wanted, in an instant, her tears left, her mouth turned up and she radiated happiness! Willie swears that the phrase "turn it off like a tap" fits Helen. I did not realize how the older boys played a game with her to see her change from a huge pout to a happy face in one second.

Nan remembered how Helen copied Nan's every move. If Nan crossed her legs, so would Helen. If Nan said, "more milk please", so did Helen! George remembers how Helen would tease him and then run away, and he could never catch her.

She was basking in praise and then Hugh said that I said he could have all the leftover cake. She believed him, and yest, she started her famous pout – until she caught on and her high laughter returned very quickly.

These are moments that are special, and I hope they will be retold long after Arch and I are gone.

On Saturday, Arch took me downtown to buy me my Christmas present early. It is a lady's muskrat coat. It is lined with heavy satin twill and is so long for me, it is right to the floor. It cost $69 on sale at Devitt's Fur Store. I am waiting for Christmas Sunday to wear it to Church.

December 1912 pages are full of facts and figures. Now they make a lot of little charts. Of course, they always show growth, never declining figures or store closings. The statistics for 100 cases of Typhoid this year, with 12 deaths, are shown in the following chart.

Causes of Typhoid		
Cause	Cases	Deaths
Wells (water)	26	3
Flies	35	4
Milk	18	4
Infestation	11	
Imported	11	1

I think these charts help citizens to see and understand reasons. This chart was followed by some astounding figures. By the end of October, the inspectors had made

4,118 inspections. Reports of some basements are horrible. 158,000 lbs. of contaminated meat were found. Conviction and fines for trying to sell contaminated products are $95 for each offence.

Arch saw the advertisement for the new Studebaker. Three different models are priced between $1,050 and $1,800. Of course, they have electric starters plus many other features.

Closing out figures for 1912 were reports on the hospitals. City Hospital took care of 1,600 patients. St. Paul's treated more than 1,000. City has 16 graduate nurses and St. Paul's has 18. Can you believe it? One has to book an appointment two to three weeks ahead! In an effort to keep up, City Hospital will be replaced in 1915 and St. Paul's will build a 4 storey hospital to be ready next September.

The report is that 1,400 new houses were built in 1912.

1913

January 7, 1913

We had a cold and quiet Christmas.; the usual food and drinks! I made a lot of mincemeat tarts this year. We like them better than the pie. I have tart tins that are very small and fluted. It is a lot of work, but they are a big favourite. Hugh calls them "two bites" but the older boys' mouths are so big they can pop a whole one in at a time.

We decided not to give each person an individual book, but we got books to share. Willie likes adult books and Geordie now reads all the books that the older ones read a few years ago. The girls loved their shared books. They are in love with "The Story Girl" by L. M. Montgomery and "The Secret Garden" by Frances Hodgson Burnett. "Chronicles of Avonlea" rated high, and, of course, "Anne of Green Gables".

Willie had discovered Jack London, the pseudonym of John Griffith Chaney, so we went overboard on his books, but they were all a good price: "Call of the Wild", "White Fang", "Martin Eden", "The Sea Wolf", "The Iron Heel", "The Star Rover". For ourselves, we really indulged! "How We Think" by John Dewey and "Twenty Years at Hull House" by Jane Addams. Arch and the boys will enjoy Booker T. Washington's "Up From Slavery".

Hugh and Jim are already into Zane Grey's books: "The Lost Trail", "The Spirit of the Border", "Riders of the Purple Sage". As for me, I like Ralph Connor (perhaps because he is a Presbyterian minister). We added "The Doctor", "The Foreigner", about Saskatchewan and "The Recall of Love".

I was shocked when our list was tallied. We picked 20 books, but Arch is looking forward to taking a book on the road.

We spent a lot on new sweaters and sweater coats for everyone, but I had watched for sales all fall. The girls are almost over wanting toys and there are lots around for Geordie.

January 27, 1913

We had the usual Robbie Burns' Day supper at the church (Westminster). Last year we took Hugh, so this year we took Willie – now he wants bagpipes! Mrs. McDonald made all the haggis this year and it was very tasty.

At the end of last year, the newspaper was starting to promote a huge new project. Billy Silverwood owns many acres just north of town. His milk was highly sought after and there was a natural spring on his property – good for water and beer. Some top investors from the East are bringing in an ambitious plan for a whole new "city". So far this year, there has been a report of new development for Factoria. One can tell by the tone and frequency of ads in the newspapers that the promotion tactics are wordier and more sophisticated than local ones. The first project, already started, is a 3 storey hotel with 66 rooms. Almost ready is a bunkhouse for 40 carpenters working on the hotel. Already sites are spoken for. Lot #1 will be a brewery. Lot #2 will be Hollow Brick Tiles Factory. #3 is a plant for building Trussed Walls that will make 12 thousand trussed bricks daily. Sandline Brick Factory will be on Lots 4, 5 and 6.

It was announced that a factory to make stove pipes has started and will be finished in the fall. The plan is for 300 men to be employed. It was just reported that 20 acres of river frontage between Saskatoon and Factoria has been purchased by The Gratias Land Co. The price was $700 per acre. The CNR is laying tracks at Factoria. As soon as they are laid, 1,000 carloads of material will arrive. A prediction has been made that Factoria will have a population of 2,000 by the end of 1913.

Aside from Factoria news, January was a busy month. The annual Curling Bonspiel happened. Teams from other towns were here. Arch loves to curl, but being out of town, it is not possible for him to curl on a regular team, so he was to be a spare and he got lots of curling in. Willie curled with a group of lads from the High School.

The Western Canada Sawmills has been built 3 blocks from the hotel site. It was built in 15 days to furnish lumber. Three carloads of machinery from Chicago were brought in for a brick plant on blocks 66 and 67. There are so many reports that I may not have these facts in order!

February 1, 1913

We planned a different birthday for Hugh's 16th birthday. We invited some friends of both boys for an evening of games and music. Hugh's best friend, Lyle Gustin, was first choice. Eddie Mather, Glen Headly, Joe Wilhelm, Cliff McConnell and Harry Madill added to the fun. They played various card games – some are learning to play Bridge – and surprisingly, the old Crokinole board was used. We served bottles of soda (two each), popcorn, assorted nuts, ending at 10 o'clock with birthday cake and ice cream. Any food is popular with boys of all ages!

We had some newer records for the Victrola. Both Lyle and Eddie are very musical and they all joined in. Our boys are not soloist types but have good "choir" voices. Lyle made our piano sing! He played "Alexander's Ragtime Band". He is so gifted.

It was agreed that Jim should act as the host and that I would stay upstairs out of sight with the girls and Geordie. Jim adds a flair to whatever he does. The older boys in the neighbourhood quite like him, so when they got around to singing, to his delight, he was included.

When the guests all left, I went downstairs to clean and do the dishes, but Jim said that was part of his job and they chased me back upstairs. Of course Willie and Hugh pitched in. It will be one of my best memories to hear the boys singing as they worked.

February 9, 1913

Another big event for the city was the streetcars. I don't understand why they picked January 1ˢᵗ, but the first streetcar tried to make its first run to St. Paul's hospital. However, it had snowed, and they had scores of men out shovelling the tracks. On January 4ᵗʰ, Streetcar #3 was at the top of Nutana Hill and was held up for half an hour until a supervisor arrived. The driver was afraid to start down the hill on damp rails, so sand was sprinkled on the tracks. Then, by January 8ᵗʰ, they had to install a guard rail at the corner by the long hill.

Council has made a ruling that firemen, policemen and health officials can ride fee while in uniform.

Apparently, complaints were coming in about the streetcar drivers. As if they didn't have enough to do, keeping the cars on the tracks, they were advised by a poster that part of their job was to be obliging to passengers, especially the elderly, helping them on and off the cars.

Yesterday, Streetcar #7 crashed into #12, which was turning on 2ⁿᵈ Avenue to go west. All cars on 2ⁿᵈ

Avenue are to yield to traffic going west. The driver on #7 needs to learn the rules!

I think they are foolish to be trying to use the street-cars in winter. Most people are used to walking and if they can't walk, they stay home! I don't think I will try them until the snow is gone.

Other major news was the opening of St. Paul's Church which took a year to build. The inside is made of marble and the altar is 26' high and 14' wide! The finishing touches on Knox Presbyterian and Third Avenue Methodist churches are being made.

Here it is the end of February. It has seemed to be a very long month. My life seems to go on and on, on the same path. The most excitement is on wash day when I have to juggle to dry washing. I now have three clothes racks. I keep two in the basement full time and I bring the third one up to the kitchen. I have a system that I wash the sheets from half the beds one week and then the other half the following week. I can handle just so many, especially in the winter.

On February 25th, the Library opened in the Odd Fellows Temple's basement. The Saskatoon News Agency has a year's contract to supply newspapers and magazines.

February seems to be the month to plan for spring activity. The site for the 23rd Street bridge was picked and the Y.M.C.A. building will be ready by April. Also plans are to build 25 brick houses on Broadway, costing $4,500 each. More reports about development at Factoria are surfacing. The first family moved in. A huge icehouse has been completed next to the CNR yards. It is to be filled with 250 tons of ice.

The population of Canada is 7,206,643 with Quebec at the top with just over 2 million people. The Northwest Territory has only 18 ½ thousand.

March 1913

On March 11, the new Cairns store on the corner of 2nd Avenue and 23rd Street was opened. Over 12,000 people attended over a couple of days. At one point, they had to get inspectors in to see if the weight limit had been exceeded. It was fine.

April 1913

On April 15, thousands went to the River to see the ice go out. Arch was home so he took all the children in the car to see it. The three boys scrambled out and walked home.

More streetcar drama. On the corner of Avenue E and 25th Street, there is a steep curve. Children were playing in the road. The conductor rang his bell but one child didn't move so the motorman leaned over the front and scooped the child up.

On April 15 the papers were filled with stories of the sinking of the Titanic one year ago. This was the last day that claims could be filed at the U.S, District Courthouse. The damage total is $8 million. 89 claims totalling $2,216,000 were filed.

Excavations on Drinkle's two new blocks have started. The smaller one should be finished in two months. It is 75' x 130', with 3 storeys, to cost $60,000. When they advertised for workers, over 100 showed up, but they selected only 25. Mr. Drinkle is to build a third building on 3rd Avenue. It is similar in footprint size but will be 6 storeys high. I am reassured to hear they are using structuralized steel columns.

The Quaker Oats opened with elevators etc. This will double the output and will employ 60 more men. (Maybe some of the men who applied at Drinkle's blocks will find employment. The figures for this business shows that outside money is taking over in the city. This is the 11th mill owned by the same company. The only other one in Canada is at Peterborough, with

8 scattered across the U.S. and even one in Hamburg, Germany. $300,000 was spent on mill machinery.

Locally, the Y.M.C.A. opened.

I think the best thing that will benefit both the city and rural folk is the Forestry Farm with its 75,500 trees. 15,200 Acid Leaf, 33,760 Red Willow, 27000, Russian Poplar and 2,000 Caragana. We won't be considered a bald prairie 25 years from now!

The boys are hardly ever home as they are playing sports with their friends. Of course, Jim has his paper route, but Hugh takes it over if Jim wants to do something else.

More building is going on at Factoria. A power line was put to the Northland Milling Co. He needs 250 horsepower for his mill. Then building at Saskatoon Trussed Wall has started. Seven factories are secured for Factoria.

May 2, 1913

Yesterday was Nan's 13th birthday. Girls are so much harder to find gifts for. Boys always want new sports equipment. She is past dolls and paper dolls, so we are going to start giving the girls a piece of better jewelry. She was thrilled with her locket. We gave her money to invite four friends to go to Broadway for ice cream milk shakes. Helen was included. Her friends brought her small gifts like a fancy handkerchief. Another had made her a lovely bookmark. Her brothers gave her an autograph book. I didn't know if she wanted us to sign it, but she did! I wrote:

> Life is like a path
> of freshly driven snow.
> Be careful how you tread it,
> for every step will show.

Jim wrote a snappy one:

> 2 Y's U R
> 2 Y's U B
> I C U R
> 2 Y's 4 me.

Bowman Brothers brought in some Cleveland Bicycles. They are much lighter, stronger and speedier.

Arthur Rose Cleaners advertise cleaning clothes, furs, plumes, curtains and drapes and even rugs. A catchy slogan is on all their advertising: "If Rose cleaned it, it's C-L-E-A-N"

Two new buildings are reported. One is the Webb block on 4th avenue. 12 suites will be ready in September. There are 6 – 4 room suites and 6 – 5 room suites.

Also, the Farley Building on the northeast corner of 4th and 26th Street, will build 22 suites which are to be very roomy. It will be 3 storeys high and is supposed to be absolutely fireproof.

May 27, 1913

We went to the Saskatoon Symphony. We went mainly because Willie's friend played. Harry Mather was playing the trombone. I was glad I wore my best dress as so many were elegantly dressed.

Arch and his colleagues with his car.

Arch entered the Monster Automobile Parade on Dominion Day. We decorated his car with blue ribbons and a sign. There was a Union picnic at Factoria. We went out after the parade was over. We didn't stay long as it was very crowded.

The newspaper also reported that the MacMillan Department Store will open in a few weeks, but the biggest news of building projects will definitely be The Canada Building. Built by Allan Bowerman, it is 8 storeys high and the interior is done in marble and oak.

I was so focused on all the building in the city, I forgot to tell of a debate Willie went to at Christ Church. Willie envisions himself as a potential great debater. The men's social at Christ Church set it up. The topic: "Should women be kept away from polling booths?" The affirmative strongly supported this idea. Willie was shaking his head by the way the debated topic was worded and to the fact that no women were even present!

Another streetcar incident that caused some humour. Conductor Hugh Eaton forgot and was leaning out the side window. The trolley had come off and instead of getting out, he tried to do it from inside! Hence some more rules added.

July 4, 1913

It is hard to believe that Willie has turned 18 and Jim 15! We had to make a lot of important decisions, particularly about Willie. He graduated with his Junior Matriculation but could not fix on one thing he wanted to do. After a long discussion, "we" decided he should go back to the Collegiate for another year to get his Senior Matriculation. Very few choose to do that, but it opens so many more doors. Also, he needs to apply himself and get better grades. Arch came up with a new idea. If by spring, he is getting good grades, for his 19th birthday, we will buy him a Harley-Davidson motorcycle from Walter's Cycle. I think it is somewhat like a bribe but Arch calls it an incentive.

It may seem like a strange birthday present, but we decided both boys – and Arch – needed a better raincoat. I found them on sale for $8 each, regular $15. So really, we got one for free. Surprisingly, both boys were pleased as they are proper adult coats.

August 1913

Another report about the riverbank! They say by the long hill, it is sliding into the river. A few weeks ago, the earth gave way underneath the road and sidewalk.

There were long cracks, so using teams of horses, earth was used as a temporary measure.

We were going to let the girls go to the Fair this year but were worried it would not be safe. CNR actually brought in 36,000 people in the four days. The boys admitted it was too big and too busy.

What a shock. The headline in the newspaper read "Dr. McKay former MHO of Saskatoon passed away in London". He left his parents' home in Morden to go to London to take a special course in hospitals. Enoch said John spent some time with Hartford and Margaret, but they are now a part of a family. While John loved them, he just wasn't the kind of man to be a good single father and he had no interest in marrying again. He is driven and puts every ounce into his profession.

For some reason, thinking about his life, I know his passion was people and their welfare. Compared to Arch, his focus was on others, while Arch measures himself by a different yardstick. For Arch, his world is his family. While Arch cares and serves others, he measures his success by his family.

John measured his worth by saving others and so family was not enough. I suppose the world needs both kinds of men, but John certainly made a big impact on so many lives, even those who are not aware of his deeds.

The plans for the funeral are still being arranged.

Just a week later, the Star reported that 16 babies died of infant cholera in the past three weeks. This was an issue that Dr. McKay was passionate about, educating about contamination of milk by dirty places, flies and dirty bottles. While trying to reconcile this statistic as a loss (and it is), I remind myself if the Doctor had not been here in the earlier days, those figures would have been double or triple now.

I just could not make a cheery entry, but to get my mind off John's death, I will copy some interesting figures from the newspaper.

For the months of March, April, May and June, these are the totals:

Births – 4,776

Marriages – 1,611

Deaths – 1,443

September 1913

On September 6, the announcement for Dr. McKay's funeral was made. The paper reported he died in London, England, but actually he was on a motorcycle holiday in Ireland when he was struck. Arrangements were made with CNR for a special car to take members of City Council, the Masonic Order and other friends to Morden. Arch, of course took time to go. He did not come home with the others, as he stayed a few extra days to visit with family. My sister – the Enoch Winklers – had him stay in their beautiful home. They took him to see the twins a day after the funeral. Hartford and Margaret are doing so well, and although it seems strange to say, the trauma of John's death will not be as great if they were a few years older. The funeral was one of the largest Arch has ever been to. Dr. McKay touched many lives in so many ways.

Life goes on, and so, on a cheerier note, 4,000 people saw our Quakers defeat Robin Hood 7 – 2 in Prince Albert.

When school opened, the public schools were short 300 school desks. Some classes have enrolments of 60 pupils. 60% of the school population is under 12 years old. Since our children started 5 years ago, the whole tone of education has lost a lot of connections individually between teacher and student. The estimate for pupils in schools is 3,200, with 350 new pupils. The most overcrowding is at Caswell, Victoria and Princess.

To help out at Victoria, they moved the boundary and grades 3 – 5 will go to Albert School.

I ventured over to 20th Street for a huge sale at F. R. Bailey & Co – under new management. I took my large tapestry bag and it was full! Here are some of my purchases. Some I will give as gifts, or for the girls.

> Celluloid hair combs, 4 per card, regular $10, paid $4
>
> Back side combs, regular 40¢ a set, paid 16¢
>
> Large fancy celluloid hair pins, regular 20¢, now 2¢ Pearl buttons, regular 10¢ a card, now 2 cards for 9¢ Safety pins, paid 2¢
>
> Red Cross hairnets (I like these for myself), regular 3 for 25¢, now 4¢ each

The paper of September 9th reported great crops of 30 – 40 bushels per acre. 46 cars of wheat were loaded yesterday but there is still a good supply of empties. A farmer 6 ½ miles north of the city got 25 – 35 bushels per acre (no. 1 Northern). ½ ton of binder twine was used.

Coincidentally, around the same time as John McKay's funeral, there was a report that Maddock Milk Co. will build a plant. Brand new equipment will provide the city with milk that has been pasteurized. All milk will be heated to 148° for 3 minutes. Then cooling pipes take it down to 36°, or just a little above freezing. They will have two horses making daily deliveries. Dr. McKay fought hard to supply cleaner milk.

September 30

A very important event was explained thoroughly in the paper. The article was an incentive for Willow following his Senior Matriculation. Details about the 3 year program leading to a Bachelor of Law degree were outlined. The college will open with four professors – Moxon, MacKay, Shannon and the Hon. T. H. McGuire – with assistance by members of the local bar. The basic qualifications are Matriculation, evidence of a good moral character and be at least 17.

For the first 2 years, the lectures will be planned, for the convenience of students, in offices. They outlined topics presented for each year. Year 1 will be Constitutional History, Contracts, Torts, Real Property, Criminal Law and Evidence. In between, students will work in a Law Office. Examinations will be held in May and November. On top of lectures, students must submit papers on prescribed topics. First year has five papers; year 2 must present 7 papers and the 3rd and final year, they must prepare 8 papers.

Another full report on grades and classification is very helpful to me. Starting at the beginning, a Standard I is the first year, II – second year and so on. On Report Cards, Class I is 66% or higher. Class II is between 55% and 66%. Class III is below 50. Also teaching certificates were explained. The classifications are Third Class (less that complete high school; also called Provisional), Second Class Provisional, First Class and Superior First Class. Many young teachers go out to rural schools with Third Class Provisional ranking.

I forgot to report some interesting facts that somehow pertain to our family's interests. On September 15, J. Walters had a Harley-Davidson single in races and a Harley-Davidson twin. Willie and Hugh attended and came home very excited. From the beginning of the season, there were 35 more machines in the city. Bowman Bros. are the agents for Indian motorcycles, but Willie is already dreaming of 'his Harley".

Also, Arch's brother P. J. served on the jury of Doris White's murder conviction of her husband. They eventually found her guilty of manslaughter. Of course, P. J. could not discuss it, but he said he found it a heavy burden.

I think I have found my preferred way of shopping. The Saskatoon Trading Co. had some specials and offered free delivery every day. By phone, I placed a large order:

Basket of pears - $1.25

2 baskets of apples - 75¢ each

Choice preserving plums - $1.25

2 x 17 lb. potatoes for 25¢ - 50¢

5 lb. tin of Pure Fruit Raspberry jam - 65¢

20 lb. sack of sugar - $1.10

6 boxes Shredded Wheat - 10¢ each

2 orders of Grape Nuts that were 2 for 25¢, so 50¢

3 dozen fresh corn for 45¢

That totalled $7.80, so I added some baking – an apple pie and a raisin pie at 25¢ – so I got all that for under $10. The baking was actually quite good, although my pie crusts are better.

In several September papers, a sketch artist and cartoonist, C. Stafford, had some wonderful drawings for Wentz, Duncan McCallum, Mayor Fred Harrison, Neville Garrett, C.H. Pruner, Drinkle.

So, September was a busy month. All the children have settled into a routine. Some classes have too many pupils.

October 1913

October 10 Geordie's 9th birthday! He has wanted to go for some entertainment at night, preferably at the Empire. So we gave him a "promissory note" for a suitable show in the future. Maybe I don't have my old enthusiasm for birthdays. However, he seemed satisfied with a special family supper.

On the subject of Geordie, he has made a new friend, Fred Whittaker. Fred's father, Arthur, is the janitor at the Collegiate. They live just across from the Collegiate. Their house is very similar to ours. Fred is like an only child as he has only one sister that is much older. I think the boys are similar in nature, although Fred is already a fine athlete. He has Geordie out playing soccer. I would say that Fred is Geordie's first real friend. I hope their friendship lasts for years.

October 20, 1913

St. Paul's hospital opened today. It accommodates 100 patients with about 35 nurses. Some of the funds were raised by public subscriptions, showing citizens recognizing the need.

October 31, 1913

Geordie chose a belated birthday gift. "Freckles" was presented at the Empire for only last night. I said he could choose who would be invited. I was surprised when he chose me – he said I am hist first and best friend. He chose Helen and Nan and also his new friend, Freddie Whittaker. The seats, purchased in advance, ranged from 25¢ - $1.25. I chose the 75¢ ones and they were lovely.

Earlier I had invited Mrs. Whittaker over for tea one afternoon so she would know more about Geordie. I quite like her! We are both of a quiet nature and there is no pretense on the part of either of us, so I guess I have a new friend also.

Rounding out the month of October, there were reports about "The Sheaf" – the first publication of the student paper at the University. The Editor is J. W. Cruikshank and the business manager for ladies is Miss O. Pettit. Also, Clinkskill opens his two new adjoining stores on 2nd Avenue. The Caledonian Pipe Band played for two hours, while hundreds of people showed up.

November 1913

I wonder what is going on. There was an actual Bankruptcy sale at King Edward Clothing Co. Usually the ads just say "closing sale" but this one is run by the National Trust. $34,000 of stock was offered. Then on November 19 the Bankruptcy sale of E. Bowman, managed by Everly Sales Co. of Calgary $18,000 worth of stock for sale.

December 1913

On December 3rd and 4th, the Saskatoon Oratorio Society presented "Messiah" at the Methodist Church. There were 200 performers. We went on the second night. What wonderful uplifting music!

In about a month, the White Steamer Motor Coo. Of Cleveland will establish a taxi service with 6 White Steamer cabs for hire. Also, 2 new streetcars have arrived with 4 more coming. The total charge for the 6 is $28,120, or $6,687 each. On a down note, 11 street railway men were charged with stealing from the fare boxes. Two charged that we know slightly are Alex Mather and B Covey. Shame.

The year-end statistics for the University of Saskatchewan were published. There are a total of 322 student, including 106 students in Agriculture, 55 in 1st year Arts and Science and 31 in second year. The article also gave the ethnic and religious breakdown of the students. In Agriculture, there were 34 Canadians, 25 English, 14 Scottish as well as few from other backgrounds – for example, Germans – 7. The religious figures reflected similarities. 16 were Anglican, 39 Presbyterians, 30 Methodist, 1 Baptist, 1 Roman Catholic and 4 Lutherans.

December 31, 1913

So ends the year 1913 – with a Grand Concert and supper on New Year's Eve at J. F. Cairns café. Tickets were $1 each and it was Jim's turn to come with us. He loves anything Scottish – food, pipes, dancing. It was a wonderful programme with pipes and soloist Robert W. C. Fyfe. He and his wife rendered "How Come Ye Gang Laddie" and "Come Under Ma Plaidie". Neil Black was a hit with his comic song "It's Nice To Get Up in the Morning". He also sang "It's a Wee Dochen Doris". Robert Wilson did an amazing display of club swinging. He was the champion in Scotland in 1910 and 1911.

We give thanks to the Lord for all the good things of 1913 and courage and peace to face the "not so good".

1914

January 12, 1914

We had a wonderful beginning of the New Year by attending a party at J. F. Cairns store. My brother Jim and his wife Kate came with us. They hesitated to leave Caroline home alone with young Mac, so the two children slept over at our place. Caroline is Helen's age, but a very serious child. She excels at Piano and dance. The cousins don't see a lot of each other – we should make more effort. Wee Mac is Geordie's age. Our Geordie is quite serious while Mac is a bit of a rascal. Willie and Hugh thought he was so much fun. Then Jim and Kate came over New Year's Day. Brother Jim always makes me think of our family and what fun we had when we were children in Manitoba. In fact, I sat down and wrote long letters to my sisters Maggie, Marry, Helen and Alice. They all married well and their children are all grown up.

When Willie started his final year of high school last fall, he decided he needed a more mature sounding name. He wants us to call him William. He thinks it will sound better when he becomes a lawyer. So every time someone calls him Willie, he corrects them. Of course, Geordie will call him Willie Winkie and runs away with Bill chasing him. I think the decision to stay in school another year was the right one. Bill's marks are up, and he actually studies for tests now.

Hugh turns 17 on the 29th. Unfortunately, his marks do not get better.

Oh yes, for Christmas gifts, we broke our rule about not giving too much. Everyone needed new clothes, especially the three older boys. They do look smart in their new suits of the latest style. I hired a dressmaker to make the girls new outfits. I know they are spoiled with new dresses but I want them to be the best dressed girls at school. Arch got a new suit also.

At the beginning of 1913 the newspapers were filled with glowing reports of the wonder city, Factoria. No so much now! One article this January refers to the tightness of the money market in the old country.

At City Council on January 31st, a new schedule of salaries was disclosed. The Mayor will get $4,000 a year. The Commissioner receives $5,000, Secretaries average between $1,000 and $2,000. Stenographers are underpaid at ranges between $660 and $900 per year. Most stenographers are female and live at home.

February 1914

Late February and more reports of trouble in Paradise (Factoria) are emerging. The Commissioner wants Council to state conditions on the request to lay a power line to Factoria. The city wants Billy Silverwood to guarantee that Factoria will use a certain amount of power yearly. There was not much of a response, so the new plan is for the city to build a line carrying 1,000 kilowatts to the powerhouse three miles north of the city. Factoria is to share costs of construction from the powerhouse to Factoria. Further delays. Silverwood claims the cable would have to come from England. Finally, at the end of a council meeting in February, Donald McLean, representing the Northland Milling Co. said Silverwood was in England now, but off the record, McLean said he knew Silverwood could not meet the requirements the city was asking.

March 1914

At the Marc 14th Council meeting, the Parks Board cut $3,000 out of their $23,000 budget. "Tightening the belt is the new operative rather than the reckless "expansion of the belt" seen in the last few years.

Arch tells me not to worry as the new Studebaker car is out, so the economy must be sound. It has electric lights and starter, left handed steering with controls in the middle. $1,315 up to Six Sedan for $2,900. I reminded him he had promised Bill a motorcycle for his birthday in July.

April 1914

Maybe Arch is correct and some of my earlier fears are alleviated by all the activity happening. The Woolworth Co. of New York opened a store in the MacMillan Building on 2nd Avenue. They operate 60 5¢ - 10¢ stores in Canda and U.S. Buena Vista School opened with 6 rooms and 180 pupils. The old temporary room next to the new building will be used by the Normal School students. They had been at the Collegiate, but the Collegiate needed the room back. The Quaker Baseball Club is selling coupon books for the season. The 40 game coupon book is selling for $10. The Saskatoon Country Club plans a new clubhouse for $10,000.

The largest and most expensive building is the grain elevator, worth $1,250,000. The storage capacity is 1 million bushels. 1,000 piles were sunk to support it. The capacity is to be able to receive 13 cars of grain per hour and to ship out 24 cars full. It should be ready for the Fall crop of Western Canada.

There was a picture of the new Y.M.C.A. It cost $750,000 to build and already has 1,000 members. Several lads got up on top of the various roof levels for the picture. The Aberdeen Fish Market boldly advertised the sale of 60 fat, young, freshly killed rabbits for sale today for 25¢ each! I think most will be sold on the Westside. I doubt if a rabbit, fresh or not will be served on a Nutana table.

The MacMillan Store has a 30 foot long operating model of the Panama Canal. It was here one week, and arrangements were made by schools to view it. Teams work on the long hill to remove 75,000 cubic feet of earth.

There is a dog issue – dogs are to be tied up or muzzled by law. A cute cartoon in the paper was of a muzzled man, with the caption "30 days is a long time for a fellow to keep his mouth shut." The new Baseball Park on Avenue A opened. There are 1,400 seats and cost $12,000 to build. The boys all went and loved it. A long way from ball at a little country school.

City Council reports $3,000 will be spent on new sidewalks. A few years ago, they were all about building concrete sidewalks. Now they are laying plank sidewalks, which are cheaper. Further, they will lay them on only one side of the block. An example – on 32nd Street, west from Avenue F (streetcar stop) to Avenue H on the north side of the street.

May 1914

The end of May was taken up with garden planting. Bill and Hugh "need" to study, so they disappear. Jim would love to use the same play, but we remind him that he never studies! He does the heavier work with a little help from Geordie. The girls help me with the flowers and Helen loves mowing the grass.

Last Sunday, the new Knox served communion to 450 people. We went and it was a lovely service. The interior is spectacular, but Arch is still not convinced that all that grandeur is pleasing to God. Rev. Wylie Clark's message was on "Remembrance". Somehow one concept that speaks to me is fear: fear of forgetting and fear of being forgotten. Forgetting seems to happen to a lot of females on the Stewart and McKeith lines so I "fear" that fear may come real for me. However, the fear of being forgotten moves me. I do not forget our ancestors, but I worry this young generation will not be into remembering the past or me. My thought is that maybe memories of me will not be passed on to grandchildren and great-grandchildren. I wish some will remember me as a person, not just as a mother or wife. Sometimes even now, I feel I am not really seen as me!

Arch planned a trip for the four boys. He took them out of school for a week to go to the farm. They left Monday morning and got to Marsden before the stores closed. I sent along everything I thought they would need but Arch wanted to show off his four sons. They took lots of food and baking, plus a bowl, cup and cutlery for each person. I gave them old sheets, blankets and towels. Hugh took his kit that he has for camping with the Boy Scouts.

Our farm neighbours, the Rutherfords, rent our land. They are so kind and friendly. They have two boys around the ages of our older boys, and they took great delight in showing the city slickers around. Mr. Rutherford let his boys use one horse and light wagon. The Rutherford boys showed our boys how to fell a couple of trees, cut them up and chop them and haul the wood home. There will be a good supply of dry wood the next time anyone goes there.

Arch took off in the car on Tuesday, Wednesday and Thursday while our boys were shown around the countryside and learned what chores are! Bill loved the horse as it reminded him of the one we had in Morden.

We were surprised that Hugh was the one who fell in love with it all. He claims he will make it his place to retire to. Jim and Geordie love the experience but decided they would stay "city boys".

The Rutherfords had them to supper 3 times and provided them with milk and eggs. Such kind "neighbours"!

Arch didn't go to work on Friday, while the boys, now knowing lots, showed off their new knowledge and skills. They left for Saskatoon on Saturday and arrived home dirty, hungry and with many enthusiastic stories. Nan showed little interest, but Helen was really put out that she was not allowed to go.

Another tragedy at sea! On May 28th, the CP mail liner, "RMS The Empress of Ireland" was in collision with "The Storstad", a collier carrying tons of coal. 1,000 souls perished in the St. Lawrence. (I don't know why reports always say "souls" perished. The bodies perish, but souls should live on!) 450 survivors were picked up. The casualty is so great when a huge ship such as the Titanic sinks.

June 5, 1914

A report on the new organ installed at Knox Church. The price was $10,000 for the Casavant organ. It is a Three Manual, with 42 stops: 14 are swell stops, 8 stops are on the choir organ and 11 on the great organ. 2,683 pipes issue magnificent, majestical music. No everyday pianist could master the complexity. Even some of the better known players have to stick to playing their grand pianos while mediocre players, (like Helen and me) plunk away on our uprights.

June 20, 1914

We attended the I. F. Cairns picnic. 500 people attended. Even that seems like a lot of people, but it still had the feeling of a small town or Church picnic. The races were fun to watch. Douglas Lawson won the slow bicycle race while Olive Wagner won the ladies' "threading the needle". The most popular race was the wheelbarrow race. A very light Mrs. Hardy was pushed by a burley Mr. Burton. Olive Wagner also won the "Fast Ladies' Race". The gentlemen's boot race was won by the team of Mr. Smart and Len Hillyard.

June 30. 1914

Headlines in the paper were about Archduke Ferdinand and his wife shot at Sarajevo. I had no idea where Sarajevo even was – and who was the Archduke – and of what? Bill exclaimed "Here comes trouble!" When Arch came home on Friday, together Bill and Arch patched together this information for me to better understand the situation. Apparently, several smaller countries in kind of lower Europe were lumped together loosely and referred to as "The Balkans". Earlier, the Ottoman Empire had fought against the four Balkan States of Serbia, Bulgaria, Croatia and Albania. To the west and a little north was Austria-Hungary. This was started when Austria-Hungary issued an ultimatum to Serbia to stop dangerous propaganda.

July 2, 1914

Bill Munro.

An exciting day today! Bill got his long awaited motor-bike! It is a Harley-Davidson from Walter's Cycle Shop. Arch arranged for it to be delivered. They sent two men, one on their bike and one driving Bill's. They went over it, explaining how it all worked and then they waited until Bill tested it and drove around for quite a while. We were impressed with the service. They also gave for free, a high pair of laced leather boots and a pair of driving gloves. The boots are vital because of heat given off. Bill's first passenger, after he mastered how to handle it, was Jim who turned 16! Huch wasn't interested and said he'd rather walk – and stay alive! Jim pointed out that Hugh could die if Bill accidently drove over him!

August 1914

By August 1st, the paper said that CNR will carry most of the Austrians who want to return to their homeland to join in the war. CNR will take them to Montreal.

On August 3rd, our headlines read

GREAT BRITAIN AT WAR
All but the formal declaration

The headline on August 4th was:

WAR IS DECLARED

King George tried to make a final effort to stop the war, but Sir Edward Grey of the House of Parliament said "fight!".

The next day, the paper headlined

GERMANY DECLARES WAR ON BELGIUM
Martial Law Is Proclaimed in Great Britain.

August 5th headline:

Great Britain Declares War against Germany
and the Navy is ordered to strike at once

For me, this does not seem real. The young people are playing tennis and going to the Exhibition. What is Happening? However, on August 7, 105th Regiment is asking for volunteers. Recruiting is at the Armory. The Frontiersmen are to have a parade to encourage enlisting. They hope for up to 1,000 men to respond (but all will have to pass a physical and mental assessment). Then the Highland Pipe Band paraded with 42 men.

Items from the newspaper on August 8th:

- 10 of the City Hall staff have enlisted.

- Naval Reserve men leave for coast

- 63 Frontiersmen to leave on August 14th

- Canada to send 20,000 men

- Belgians and French show vigorous force
  on Germany.

On August 14th, they reported that the Post Office has cut off all mail to Germany, Austria, Hungary and Luxembourg.

How quickly things change, even in Saskatoon. There are people here from many different countries. Only a year ago we were singing the praises of our fine German residents. Now, hatred for an unknown "enemy" is spilling over into everyday life. Our friends, the Oscar Wilhelms, who live down ninth street have been called names. He is a professor and now people avoid him. The two boys, Joe and Frank are friends of our children. Arch and I stressed that our boys must stand beside them if anyone makes unkind remarks. (Although I am glad we don't have the surname Wilhelm right now.)

August 17th - 200 volunteers leave for training at Valcartier, Quebec in two days.

August 19th – All local regiments escort their comrades in a parade to CP station. The same edition described how the Daughters of the Empire quickly made sewing kits. The Fusiliers 1st Battalion have

300 men and 29th Light Horse have 169, so that was remarkable to get so many kits together.

That same day paper reported that the Canadian Parliament has ordered 30,000 Ross rifles costing $33.25 each. And "we" bought a submarine from Chili for over 1 million dollars. They are also paying for the conversion of 10,000 Ross Long Rifles for $3.50 each. All these items together cost $2,100,000.

Meanwhile, life goes on in Saskatoon. The lower bank of the Long Hill has broken away causing a 30' trench. Tons and tons fell and could be heard a mile away. I fear our "war" with the long Hill is not over!

August 29, 1914

Finally Canada's first 100 soldiers to England sail on the Princess Patricia.

There was an interesting article about the Potts family. Seven sons all joined. I dread the thought of giving up even one son. So far, Bill has not made noises about joining.

September 19, 1914

I had never even thought about the Cavalry needing horses! The province hopes to provide 1,500 to be shipped overseas. A specific ad, telling what kind, size and nature of horses will be purchased by the province at fair, but cheap, prices. What a sacrifice for farmers! To part with an animal they love and depend on is heartbreaking. The horses are being gathered and housed at the Exhibition. Of course, they have to be fed and watered. Hay costs $5 a ton.

An amazing windfall was gained by Knox Presbyterian Church. Mrs. Copland's estate left Knox $20,000. Several groups, such as the Children's home were bequeathed $1,000 - $2,000. Two ministers she thought highly of – Rev. John Little of North Battleford and Rev. Wylie Clark – were each given $1,000.

October 1914

I am so caught up with the war that I forget about what is happening her. Hugh's best friend, Lyle Gustin, gave a brilliant recital at the Pennant Theatre in Sutherland. He played pieces by Brahms, Schumann, Mendelssohn, Chopin and Moszkowski.

King George school has been closed for fumigation because of a diphtheria outbreak.

The Phoenix announced that McKague's Ambulance has a great horse ambulance – 24 hour service at $3 a call. They also send a trained first-aid man and a stretcher. Horses at the ready and faster and more reliable in any weather.

The Women's Group at Westminster are getting very involved in supporting men from our Church. I find this work very rewarding and I am going out to the Church more. We were given some very important mailing instructions for the soldiers at Salisbury Plains. To mail; have name, address, regiment or brigade; send to GPO London, England, prepaid at 12¢ a lb. Then you must also have a Customs Declaration. Rates: less than 1 lbs. = 22¢; 1 – 2 lbs. = 40¢; 2 – 3 lbs. = 45¢; 3 – 4 lbs. = 48¢; 4 – 5 lbs. = 64¢; 5 – 6 lbs. = 72¢. A letter from Mr. McDonald from Salisbury Plain to his mom at 409 – 29th Street was published.

The paper also reported that Salisbury Plain will soon house 60,000 men and 15,000 horses. 33,000 will be Canadians and 25,000 Australians. There are 800 huts.

Yearend school reports show young Frank Wilhelm down the street passing to Grade VII at Buena Vista. Also nephew McKeith (Mac) Stewart was promoted to Senion 2 at Buena Vista. Nutana Collegiate has 629 pupils with 14 teachers.

December 1914

At the beginning of December, the Men's Society at Christ Church assembled about 40 parcels for men overseas. Women had made fruitcakes.

Our year at 422 9th Street ends a year of major change., but not too much for our family. Bill, at 19, has been at Law School for 4 months and loves it all. Hugh will soon be 18 and at the Collegiate. Jim is an energetic 16 ½ year old boy, also at the Collegiate. Nan turned 14 this year while Helen just turned 12. Wee Geordie is ten.

We pray earnestly that this war will end quickly and all boys will be home safely. We hope such evil will never touch our own sons.

1915

January 1915

Our Christmas was similar to many we have experienced in years past. The three older boys, particularly Bill and Hugh, are more involved in various activities away from home. Bill has played soccer for several years with the Westminster Church team, although his first love is lacrosse. Last year he took on coaching a team of younger boys. He also loves watching ball at Cairns field or City Park. Hugh is hardly home in winter as he "lives" curling, both playing and watching. Jim, like Bill, loves baseball, but he actually plays more than Bill does. All three boys have many friends they do activities with. All three love going to the movie theatres. The boys are members of Westminster Young People's Society. The group puts on song services after church.

What I really noticed this past Christmas was how much the home activities have shifted to Nan and Helen and their friends. Arch and I, for fun, started the girls playing bridge. They are funny as they try to act so grown up. The even drink tea with us! Lately the boys have shown some interest in bridge, so sometimes one of them will sit in, especially if Arch is on the road.

Bill Munro in 1915

I spend a lot of time sewing – especially outfits for the girls. They also love to cook. If he has time, Bill shows some interest. His favourite is making molasses taffy from my mother's recipes.

Hovering over our family and others is an air of anxiety and worry. Many thought the war would be over by now, but reality surfaces when the first lists of casualties were published in the papers. The ones that enlisted at the beginning were up to six months in training at Sewell. Some of the first to enlist were men who had served in past wars. Many are men who came from the Old Country to Canada in the early years.

On January 16, the caption was about the Princess Patricial Light Infantry. Apparently when they charged the Germans, often using bayonets, the cry that went up was "For Canada and Old England". Then the article said 2 were killed and 14 wounded.

Recruitment centres are more prevalent. Small towns, such as Humbolt, just sent in 50 men for the 46th Battalion. Saskatoon recruited 110 men in the city, who will be billeted at the Exhibition. Each volunteer is given a number. By the number, the unit which the person originally joined is identified. I am starting to understand the structure. There are division. 3rd Division is Western Canada, 2nd Division, Quebec and 4th Division is Ontario and the Atlantic provinces. The next level down are Battalions. The battalions will be made up of 4 – 6 companies. There could be 1 thousand men commanded by a Lieutenant Colonel.

February 1915

I have decided to write a summary each month with all news about the war. In February, the call went out for more troops. Mayor Harrison is going to Winnipeg to get Major-General Steele to say more forcefully that the Saskatoon Exhibition grounds could house up to 1,200 men. On February 4th it was reported that 158 men of "A" Squadron of the CMR moved to the Exhibition grounds from various hotels because "C" Squadron has moved on to Brandon, taking only their mattresses and blankets. New blankets for 'A' Squadron have not come as ordered so for a few days, "A" Squadron will have to get along without them. Also 170 men of the 46th Infantry will move to the Exhibition grounds as soon as equipment arrives.

I have to find a way to sometimes think of other things happening here in Saskatoon. I admire the Phoenix reporting every day local news. While these events are not much in the scheme of thing, they give us a sense of normal everyday events. We have to remember to enjoy life, sing, dance and play. But to give thanks that our country is not suffering like France or Belgium.

The February 13th paper reported that Cecil Speller, a former nurse at City Hospital was awarded the Distinguished medal. He is with the 21st Field Ambulance. His wife lives at 1026 Eleventh Street. Cecil was wounded and given only 7 days leave of absence.

February 19th, the 32nd Battalion leaves for the continent with 168 men from Saskatoon. Also, Lance Corporal Norman Fry of Netherhill and Saskatoon was one of the first Canadians to die. He served with the Princess Pats. Private Richard Herbert, who left with the first contingent of the Princess Pats was wounded.

Life in Saskatoon in February:

- St. Thomas Church presented a String Orchestra and Choir concert. The orchestra of 7 strings performed "Fantasia" by Wagner. The Bells presented a patriotic song "Hail to the Chief". Mrs. Fyfe, Mrs. Gilbert and Miss Mary Glenn sang a 3 voice trio number. There were mixed quartets and male quartets.

- Walters Cycle Shop has new 1915 models in stock that will climb a 60% grade. Many of the improvements were listed.

- J. F. Cairns moved their soda fountain from the 4th floor to the 1st. It is supposed to be the longest in Western Canada sporting two fountains.

- The Medical Health Officers reported a significant drop in typhoid in the last 8 years. In 1906, there were 197 cases and 20 deaths. 1911 saw 149 cases and 11 deaths, while 1914 had only 19 cases with 1 death.

March 1915

I will tell the highlights of reports in March. First the war news.

- 13 men were accepted in the Medical Corps with St. John's Ambulance

- Military Corps of the University of Saskatchewan is recruiting.

- Major Cheetham cabled his Dad that the 29th Light Horse reached Queensland Ireland and crossed the ocean safely.

- There will likely be two sections of the Military Corps ready to leave for Montral by April 10th. The reality is that we know several of the men either through school or Church. Some of the names that we know are Neatby, Whittingham, Caswell, Little, Smith, Hosie, Rae and Jordan.

Our family's lives have turned upside down. My brother Dan Stewart lives in Weyburn. Unfortunately, we keep in touch only by an occasional letter. Dan and his wife Annie have 7 children. The oldest boys, Chet and Roy, are about the same ages as Willie and Hugh and Cousin Jack Munro of North Battleford. Next are Bessie, Rob, Helen, Ormand and a new baby named Neil after my father. Dan is closer to Alice and so Dan sent a wire to Alice and Donald in North Battleford. Annie, Bessie and baby Neil have died from diphtheria! Donald contacted us and brother Jim Stewart. Dan contacted his sister Helan and husband Enoch Winkler in Winnipeg to let our mother Grannie Stewart know. Dan's sisters' families, Maggie Smith and Mary Sutter know. My brother Willie lives in Australia.

Enoch "took charge" of organizing and making arrangements for the Winnipeg group to come by train to Weyburn. Arch stepped up and made plans for my brother James Stewart and his wife Kate, Donald and Alice from North Battleford and us to travel by train to Weyburn. Bill and Hugh rally would have like to come but all my siblings decided that no cousins would go as it would be too overwhelming It had to be all or no one!

We took the train on Thursday morning and got to Weyburn that afternoon. Enoch had made hotel reservations for all of us. Other families might be shocked, as we decided to not get rooms as couples, but we sisters needed each other, so Grannie, Alice and myself took one room. Sisters Maggie, Helen and Mary took a room together with Kate, who was very kind to Mother. The men-in-laws managed in three other rooms. If it were not for the circumstances, Alice and I drew great strength spending time alone with our beloved mother. I hope our presence helped her.

Friday was the day of the funeral. Annie's family took charge and I so admired how they helped Dan and the children. I will always remember their kindness to all of us, because in reality, their loss was more than ours. Brother Jim was a special support for Dan as they were wee lads together. We shared our sorrow and on Saturday we found our way home – one group to Saskatoon and the other group back east to Winnipeg. Our three Saskatoon families left Dan $150 to help with expenses. I know Enoch will make sure the Winnipeg batch will help out financially also.

My Mother has three granddaughters named Helen after her. Donald and Alice's daughter Helen is 19. Our Helen is 13 and little Helen is only 10. Our Helen plans to write letters to little Helen.

April 1915

April brings more reports of the war.

After a basketball game at the Y.M.C.A., there was a little "feed" and send off for W. Nicol and V. Craighead, roomers at the Y.M.C.A. They joined the University of Saskatchewan section of McGill University Double Company. Also, James MacNab, son of Archie MacNab, Minister of Public Works, joined the 28th Battalion. Sergeant Peterson gets the Medal for gallantry for saving a man under fire. His bullet-ridden tunic is in the window of Mitchner's store.

Newspaper man Howard Wolfe of the Star Phoenix enlisted in Winnipeg and is with the first contingent to Salisbury Plain and then on to the firing line in France. His sister, Miss Wolfe, is a popular teacher at Victoria School.

There have been deaths - George Clementine near Ypres and Charles King. Lt. Burton and Pte. Ivall were wounded. Canadian casualty lists (deaths, wounded and missing) show 500 names fighting near Ypres.

They are recruiting 70 men for the 53rd Battalion and 12 University of Saskatchewan students enlisted. So far, 110 University men are overseas, including staff and students. The Faculty of Arts has the most with 17, including teacher E. Cobb. Agriculture has 12 men enlisted. Six have enlisted from the Presbyterians Theology College. Sons of England had 8 and Street Railway, 5. 13 have enlisted from the CNR and from Christ Church, 6. Two familiar lads are Alan Neatby, whose sister Hilda is in Geordie's class. Mr. Fisher, a teacher at the Collegiate, also enlisted.

Local news includes the health statistics for March – births, 84; deaths, 19.

May 1915

May brought many good things. Arch is doing his routes by automobile and Bill is enjoying his motor-cycle. He is nearing the completion of his 1st year in Law. He has a summer position clerking in a local law firm. The girls have a great group of friends. The spend hours walking to and from the houses. They often are here listening to records and having little picnics of the grass. I am glad they have happy carefree times. I wouldn't want them to focus on the war as the adults tend to do.

The biggest happening was on May 8th. The Lusitania was torpedoed. There were 2,067 aboard and only 700 survived. Not heard from are Mr. and Mrs. Henn, Miss Larking and James Woodward. Later, word came that Miss Gretta Neatby is safe in Queenstown.

On May 24th weekend, there was lots to do. The Empire Theatre was showing "The Canadian Volunteer" and the Victory Theatre showed a war drama. I cut out the baseball schedule for Jim:

- 10 am – Sutherland vrs Transporter at Cairns Field

- 2 pm – Liberals vrs Catholic Club

- 4 pm – Knox Intermediate vrs Wesley at City Park. Jim played, and of course, Knox won.

- 6 pm – Knox Juniors vrs Catholics at City Park

At the Empire Theatre at 3:45, there was wrestling – Charles Cutter vrs Jack Taylor, Champion of the World.

The lineup for football was:

- 9 am – OS vrs Thistles at City Park

- 10 am – Moose vrs CPR

- 1 pm CNR vrs 9th CMR at Exhibition Grounds.

The semi-final was at 3 pm and the final knockout at 4. At 6:30 pm St John Juniors played Westminster. Bill played.

There were also horse races, trap shooting, tennis and golf. Third Avenue Church had a picnic at Ake Lake. The I.O.D.E. had an art exhibit at the Y.M.C.A. I went to that with Mrs. Wilhelm. Finally, there was dancing at St. John's Hall, sponsored by the Tennis Club. Four female friends of Hugh and Bill's attended. Already the fact more boys are overseas is reflected.

Happy news. The Royal Confectionary Co. opened in a new shop on 2nd Avenue, to be known as "Golfs". They sell candy and ice cream and have a tearoom and bakery. Bill filled his sweet tooth as all candy sold for 30¢ a lb. Ice cream Sundaes were 10¢.

So much news about the war is published every day. It is the end of May and 18 students at the University of Saskatchewan, members of the 2nd University Company left for Camp Sewell.

Two German torpedo boats struck the 13th and 14th Battalions of Montreal. Losses were great and those two battalions no longer exist! The few survivors were transferred. Canadian casualties: 600 killed, 2,500 wounded and there are prisoners of war. A letter from a man in the 32nd Battalion told of their losses and the 29th Light Horse suffered great losses in France. The result is that more soldiers are needed.

Saskatchewan purchased 1,292 horses. The average price was $100 - $225. The total cost, $347,710.

Sad news for Saskatoon. W. Williams was killed. He worked in the local Ford Motor Co. Also, Walter Taylor was gassed. He was an active member of Christ Church and played halfback in football. He was widely known as "Chubby" Taylor. PTE. A. Eedy died of wounds and J. Davies was killed in a terrible battle on Hill 60. Bowen, of 1051 4th Street was killed at Dardanelles. Cecil Armstrong, a baseball player, was wounded. E. C. Gray, a jeweller on 20th Street was wounded. Andrew Marr, who worked at the Post Office, is wounded and missing. He was such a cheerful person.

Rev. MacIntosh of St. Thomas Presbyterian Church says 61 members have enlisted. The boys we know well are John McBain, John Denholm, William Swan, James Ball and W. Black.

Several moving letters have been published describing events. Mrs. Lambert, who has a boarding house at 112 27th Street West, reports she has had 13 enlist from her place (not all at the same time).

Meanwhile, life goes on in Saskatoon.

June 1915

War reports: Pte. Wm Sinclair (University of Saskatchewan Battalion, age 23, killed. John Robinson, 8th Battalion, killed. List of Canadian soldiers from Saskatoon are long. Harold Wilson was killed.

It seems every day there are appeals for more to enlist, both locally and Dominion-wide. The Canadian contingent will soon be 150,000. They are looking for 35,000 new recruits in Saskatchewan. Meanwhile, letters from the front inform of so many we actually know. Capt. Wm. Sage, the bookkeeper at the Strand, and Sgt. Charlie Phillips, Robert Baty, Stanley King and Roy McCutcheon have all been killed. James Ford is missing in action and Colin Weed was wounded. I know we have missed hearing about others.

It feels as if the whole town is depressed. The theatres try to bring in cheery films, but so many activities have been cancelled or slowed down.

July 1915

For the month of July, I am going to record news not related to the way to try to cheer me up.

On July 8, the Victory Theatre shoed the comedy "By the Sea" starring Charlie Chaplin. I enjoyed laughing over nothing.

The mayor declared July 14 the 1st Civic Holiday. Special trains were put on to take people to Crystal Beach at Harris. All the sporting events – baseball, football, tennis and all kinds of races were offered. They expected over 1,000 people, but only about 600 participated. Some businesses, in anticipation of the event, advertised specials. Royal Shoes had all styles of shoes for sale. Tupling had outing skirts for $1.25 - $1.75, flannel and duck trousers for $1.25 - $5.00. Middy blouses, very popular now, were $1.25 (regularly $1.75) and middy dresses, with skirt and top were $4.75. The girls got 3 middies and one skirt. I bought only one skirt – it is so comfortable and has big pockets. Nutana Bakery's specials were Snow Flake Bread (wrapped in wax paper) and picnic plates at 15¢ per dozen. Woodsides Ltd. Sold drinkables – Grape juice, 30¢ per pint, 50¢ per quart; tall lime juice or raspberry vinegar, 35¢ each. The boys took Geordie along. His fare was 55¢ return. All the boys entered in some event. Hugh mentioned how "something" was missing. We know it was so many families did not feel like going.

At the beginning of the month, the river was rising 6 feet every hour. The Crescent was under water.

The bars are officially closed – good news for the most part. 16 hotels report being affected.

The erection of the Residence Building at the University is underway. At present, there are 45 men on the construction site and Richardson says he will soon require 35 more.

The 3rd University Corps sent off 50 lads. They left from the armouries. The 1st Regimental Band under Horatio Sager led the parade. Major Trotter led 150 men of the Citizen's Corps. Bill came home very quiet. He just had his 20th birthday.

Rev. Pullinger shared this news he had received from the front. They now have goggles, respirators and smoke helmets. Often, as they march to and from the trenches, they whistle "The Maple Leaf Forever" and "O Canada".

In the July 19th paper, this advertisement read:

"Is Your Conscience Clear?
Ask yourself why are you staying at home

comfortably, instead of doing your share
for King and Country?"

This seemed to upset Bill. He suddenly announced he is taking a year off from his law studies. There is a shortage of teachers, so he signed up to teach, on a permit, at Clair, Saskatchewan. Hopefully he can sort out what he would like to do versus what he thinks he should do. Secretly, I am glad. I will miss him, but he will be in a safe place – at least for now.

We got news that Roy and Chet Stewart from Weyburn have enlisted. Annie's parents moved in to help Dan with Rob, Helen and Ormond. The two boys were too old to be instructed and too young to go it alone. Also, there was not much room in the house. Dan was a little harsh and thought they should be more motivated.

August 1915

I am writing some local news that happened this month. Of course, the "new" traffic bridge already needs some repairs. The footpath needs replacing. Two tenders were received. R. A. Dalluff bid $123 for labour only. A. W, Bell bid $507.32, all materials included. I'm not sure which one the city offered the job to!

Advertisements for farmlands show they are offered at $11 - $26 per acre, with 1/20th down and 20 years to pay. I am glad we bought our farm at Marsden last year.

The newspapers did not publish much about war casualties. I wonder why, as we know killings are still happening.

September 1915

A special show was put on at the Empire Theatre on September 1. The 65th Battalion was marched to see a film about camp Sewell. The men were led by a big band. Sometimes I think the enlistment has been painted in too-glowing colours. A lot of the lads have no concept of the grim realities of war. The marching, the uniforms, seem to take on an atmosphere of a summer camp. Reports of more casualties are appearing. George Northcote of the 32nd came home with shattered hip and almost blind.

Meanwhile, work on the student residence of the University is continuing. Its cost is $185,000 and will house 130 students.

Hugh invited me to a Lyell Gustin's recital. It was in the Sherman Theatre. He is a student of Mrs. St. John Baker. He played Sonata Opus 31 by Beethoven.

A collection was taken for the Soldier's Tobacco Fund. I gave Hugh two dollars to put in for us.

The Collegiate Principal, Mr. Pyke, told the press of the clothes left in the basement when students went out for rugby practice. The publicity pushed the School Board to promise that lockers would be installed.

November 1915

Reports of November casualties were printed. The 28th Battalion was hit by a German mine explosion. It left a trench about 20 feet deep and about an acre in area. Well known athlete Walter Glennon is reported killed., news of which was in a letter sent to Len Hunter. November's list of Canadian casualties, 19 pages, was printed. Among the names was Earl McCutcheon, 16th Battalion of 304 Avenue J North, reported to have been wounded.

Mid November the call went out for recruits for the 65th Battalion. In 2 days, 80 men were examined and right away 35 were sworn in. Out of these 35, 22 were farmers. There were 2 clerks, a court reporter, a lather, a miner, a lumberman, a surveyor, a baker, a printer, a teacher and a teamster. Of the 35, 20 were from Saskatoon.

Last year, John Cairn's Business Manager of the Phoenix and President of the Caledonian Club, was asked to raise men who want to "march to the pipes". He has raised a fine pipe band and he leaves for Winnipeg for officers' training and will start as a Private. His 18 year old son Robert is part of the group.

November's papers reported organizations who are sending packages to the troops. The University and Y.M.C.A. packages include Christmas cake, chocolates, tobacco and pipes, a copy of "The Sheaf", a tablet of soap and a special card with the University crest in the corner. The cards were signed from the Y.M.C.A., the Y.W C A. and the University of Saskatchewan. Cairn's baker made 4 – 10 lb cakes. The University boys will help with getting the gifts packed. Meanwhile, St. Thomas Church sent 90 gifts for their men in France, Rev. MacIntosh reported. St. John's Church sent slippers to the 28th Battalion.

There was a terrible slaughter of No. 19 Company. Only 10 men came back alive and 7 were from Saskatoon.

A welcome home for Pat Burns was organized by the Veteran's Society and the I.O.D.E. Burns had shrapnel in his leg and had been gassed.

December 1915

On November 30, the girls and I went to a splendid lecture at 3rd Avenue Church. I wanted the girls to hear the author of two of my favourite books and is outspoken on women's rights. Nellie McClung! I wish I had courage to speak out and maybe my daughters will follow McClung's example. I have read two of her books, "Sowing Seeds in Danny" and "The Black Creek Stopping-House, and Other Stories".

Every paper seems to report more men joining the 65th Battalion and the 96th Highlanders. The 65th had 90 applicants for enlistment. The 96th Highlanders got 13 new recruits. One was from our Church – Thomas Tait, a carpenter. The 96th go a mascot – a purebred Scotch Collie, now clad in a plaid coat. The 65th has 14 recruits, including William Brown-Baker and Alex Metcalf, carpenter.

It was good that Cairn's store had Santa Claus. It drew about 1,000 children. We should not forget the wee ones. I am getting things ready for Christmas, but my heart isn't in it. Bill will get back from Clair in time for the 25th. I just could not concentrate on shopping for gifts. Jim suggested that we give money to each of them and then they can give it to a cause of their choice. The girls and Geordie are getting one small gift. We are giving each of the girls a special bracelet and Geordie a new coat that he really wants.

When will it be over?

1916

January 1916

Christmas 1915!

It certainly wasn't a memorable one. Even though we went through the motions, it was just not the same as past Christmases.

Bill arrived home from Clair. He reported that he loved teaching. He takes pride in leading his students to think things through for themselves. He has never accepted facts without thinking about them. I think Arch is the same way to a point. Some things Arch tries to think through, yet he has the ability to accept, especially with religion and the Church. Uniformity and consistency of the church brings him comfort. He is a proud Presbyterian and seems not to question like Bill does. They have spent much time this Christmas in long private discussions. I wish I could be privy to them, but I think they just have to discuss hard topics, man to man.

Hugh was also very quiet. He spoke a little about teaching at Wadena.

The girls and Jim brought fun and laughter to the holiday season. They don't realize what a gift they have given me. I doubt somehow life will ever be the same.

On December 27, Hugh and Bill took the train to North Battleford to spend time with their cousin Jack. He wanted to talk to them. Jack is closer to Jim's age, but he seemed to need Hugh and Bill. All three boys seemed affected by their cousins Chet and Roy enlisting. Chet and Roy are overseas now. Who know what lies ahead?

Our Hogmanay was subdued. We went to Church New Year's Eve. The Westminster Kirk had special prayers for lads form the Church who are enlisted. I thought it was so meaningful that each son of the Church was name out loud. Some were:

- Alexander Wilson, the same age as Bill

- Stewart McKercher

- Alan Neatby

- Johnnie Walker

- Charles Fitzpatrick is older. He came to the city to teach. Then he started his business. His sister, Edna, is a good friend of Helen's.

Young Colin Campbell, a bright young friend was also prayed for.

February 1916

Presently 50,000 men are in Flanders, 60,000 training in England and 100,000 training in Canada. The Premier of Saskatchewan is wanting more to enlist. Every paper seems to be filled with names. Each Battalion seems to be recruiting, almost in competition. For example, the 96th Highlanders have ordered 500 kilts, specially made. Presently, 300 men are quartered in Saskatoon, P.A., N. Battleford and Yorkton. Under Col. Aitken, District #10, Area C covers the northern half of the province.

At the end of the month, all Canadian casualties, including dead, wounded and missing in action were listed by name – 16 pages of tight, small print. I made myself read every name as a small token of respect.

I needed to stop recording every event in February. So, I am just making a few entries. Denham attested to the 65th. He has 7 brothers and 3 sisters already actively engaged.

A Recruiting Committee was formed. 24 teams of two took several actions to recruit. 700 letters were sent out, resulting directly in 25 new recruits. They had special sermons preached at the Churches. I found it quite disturbing as Church should be sacred. Loyalty to King and country is noble, but it takes over from worshipping and praising God. Bill was very upset. He felt he was being preached at, with a high level of condemnation and judgment.

The next move of the committee was to visit employers to convince their employees to join. Another ploy is to publish a description of the wonderful meals. They may be serving these meals to recruits in Canada, but I doubt this will happen at the front.

March 3, 1916

I was restless and up early about 7 am. I was sitting in the parlour when Bill came into the room and shut the door behind him. "Mother, I want to tell you something – I am going to enlist tomorrow with the University 46th outfit. Telling you is the hardest because I know you don't want me to join." He said, "I can't deal with the pressure anymore. I still don't really believe a war should be on, but I know I am selfish not to join. I love my life; I love studying at the University. Others join, especially farm boys or unemployed. To them it is a way to make their lives better. I don't want to make my life better – I love it just as it is. In short, guilt is what drives me. Guilt because others are dying for us. Some say they are dying for King and Country. That is too broad a term for me. I really have examined my heart and all I feel is guilt. If I don't join, I would fee guilt forever if I did not protect and our safe, comfortable life was destroyed. Mother, may I have your support and blessing?"

I know if Arch was here, his comfort would be to turn to prayer. Instead of words, we embraced and feelings beyond words flowed between us.

Then the children came for breakfast and Bill told them He used light-hearted words and seemed to be treating it as a great adventure. Geordie was particularly excited and the girls promised to write many letters. Hugh and Jim did not say much!

March 14, 1916

Reality comes home when it is reported that Vernon Gaunt has been awarded the D.S.O. medal. Ivan

Tinkness, a local rugby player, and Harry Whitfield have both been named for the Victoria Cross.

The paper gave Saskatoon and District summaries:

- 65th Battalion – 951 men

- 96th – 475 men

- 203rd Battalion – 57 men

- University Battalion – 75 men

March 16, 1916

Dr. Munroe (no relative) was welcomed home. He joined in August 1914. He is going back in two months to run a new hospital unit. This group will have 15 officers, 18 sergeants, 6 corporals and 132 men.

The last showing of the Official Canadian Government Films of Canada's Fighting Forces was shown at the strand. The motto: "We'll Never Let The Old Flag Down". The 3 boys and Arch attended. I just couldn't bear to see it! Hugh came home all fired up to join.

March 25, 1916

Bill is now officially committed to serve in the Canada Overseas Expeditionary Force. He enlisted in the University of Saskatchewan 196th. His number is 910871.

Even though he may be transferred to other units, that number will show he enlisted in Saskatoon and with what Unit. Somehow I want to shout "My son is not a number – he is my son William McKeith Munro!"

Belle and Bill Munro in 1916 – One son off to war.

His medical examination paper recorded details I hadn't thought about for years. We used to measure their heights and record them on January 1. I remember he reached 5' by his 13th birthday and now he is 5' 7 ½", so far, the tallest in the family. He weighs 150 lbs. His eyes are grey and is hair colouring is "fair" and he is a Presbyterian. His age is listed as 20 years, 8 months.

Everyone was giddy at supper. They had even measured his chest – resting at 35" and he can expand to 37 1/2".

The paper had a catchy slogan: "Hoots mon, dae ye ken there is a war on?" The newly formed unit wants to send 3 bands, pipe, bugle and brass. Jim read the ad and said he thought Bill should have learned to play the pipes and then his chest expansion would have been greater. I am glad he expanded his head with knowledge.

April 3, 1916

A Recruiting Rally packed the Empire Theatre. Again, catchy slogans were given, such as "If You Want To Help Germany Win The War – Just Stay Right Where You Are". Canada's pledge is to provide 50,000 men.

Sgt. Tinkness, nominated for a Victoria Cross, spoke highly of German boots, which he said the British soldiers got when they got the chance. What bothers me greatly is covering the grim facts of war with catch little stories. I think some lads have no idea, or don't think of how the boots were obtained. It is not like a prize of, say, a trophy for rugby match!

Young 6 year old Jim McAllister, a bugler, played several infantry songs resulting in cheers and clapping.

April 7, 1916

The paper reports that the Civil Service of Saskatchewan. has had 174 men enlist. Now only 46 men remain on staff. Forty of them have been pronounced medically unfit. The don't say it, but the implication is that there are 6 men hiding away.

April 17, 1916

Arch told me Hugh is going to enlist in the morning. I am glad Hugh told his father first as Arch had felt a little left out when Bill joined. I find it interesting that Hugh shares little of problems with me – as he doesn't want to burden me – yet Bill has always needed to share the good and bad with me and implies that I can weather anything. I think both are right. I feel

Hugh's love, concern and his need to protect me gives me great comfort. Bill's approach to me tells me that he sees me differently – that I am stronger than I appear. I might bend at times, but I will not break.

April 18, 1916

After a sleepless night, I have had to face the fact that Hugh will be going to war also. Bill went with him to the recruiting station to show him "the drill". His medical will be done tomorrow.

April 19, 1916

Hugh's statistics are Height 5' 6 ½ ", weight 130, chest 34 ½ - 37 ½ inches. Now both boys are cleared and are waiting to be called up. Generally, they are both very excited, but they will go quiet, and I know they are asking themselves "What have I done?".

Belle Munro with Hugh and Bill in 1916.
Mothers kept giving sons to the war.

April 30, 1916

I haven't been able to think about much else as I know the day will be coming soon. But I will record a little of other news. Joe Griffith, Y.M.C.A. Sports Gym Instructor enlisted. The Young Men's Club gave him a gold watch. The staff gave him a fountain pen and the Young Ladies' Club, a signet ring.

May 4, 1916

The University Grad lists included a good representation of 9th Street boys – John Diefenbaker and Cliff McConnell. John received his Master of Arts in absentia. He enlisted, but his mother reported to me that he soon will be coming home from Camp Hughes. (Strange – she gave no reason – hoping all would assume it is for medical reasons.)

June 1916

I haven't written for a month or so. I could not bear to record more deaths. Also, too much has happened. My brother Dan in Weyburn is worried sick about his two boys, Roy and Chet. They got to England last November and now no word! Then our dear Jack lied about his age and joined up on his 17th birthday. Donald and Alice are sick about it.

If the reason was different, May 25th was a special day when Bill and Hugh got their uniforms and gear at the University. We took a set of snaps. Hugh looks like a little boy "playing soldier". Bill tried to show his independence from me when he smoked cigarettes in from of me. What mixed feelings I have. If they were off to a great adventure, such as studying abroad of starting a new career, I would be able to be excited for them. I don't want to tie any of my children to my apron strings!

Now both boys are at Camp Hughes for six months training near Carberry Manitoba. They don't write as much as I would like, but it does seem exciting. They described a huge trench system and grenade and rifle ranges. There is a huge tent city and also lots of military structures. There are retail stores, amusement complexes. They wrote that there are about 8,000 men there at any one time. Groups leave for overseas only to be replaced by a new bunch of recruits. Camp Hughes, the new name for Camp Sewell, is the largest city in Manitoba = except for Winnipeg, of course.

Camp Sewell, Manitoba in 1916.

I should be focusing more on what my other children are doing, but they are all understanding and know this is stressful for me.

Then end of June, more devastating news struck our extended family. Dan received a letter dated June 18th from a second cousin, Fitzroy McLean (Roy). Dan had copies made for each family, as it was just too much to talk about. I am including my copy here.

Belgium, June 18th, 1916

Dear Folks,

Have been back four days and have neglected writing before, because I wished to make absolutely certain regarding poor old Chet and Rex Tucker. Two companies of our battalion got blown up with a mine and only five of one Company and nine of the other, got back. Out of "B" Co., only nine got out and only one of my old pals amongst them. That morning I got back, they were parading and I stood and watched each face as they went by to see how many I knew. It's a long time since I've cried, but I'll be darned if I could keep the tears out of my eyes when I saw the remnants of the best bunch of fellows in the World.

I have made inquiries from everyone I could think of regarding Chet and Rex. The last seen of Chet was after the mines went up. He was seen going up with M.G. Crew He has not been seen since nor anyone else of the section he was with, and everyone fully believes that he is killed. Now folks, there is always the possibility that he is a prisoner, but I don't think it's possible, or at least I should say, I don't think it's probable. Poor old Chet was a general favourite throughout the battalion and was one of the few boys whom the Army didn't alter in any way. He was the same old good natured Chet through everything and was one of the "best" boys I ever knew. No matter what was on, he always had a joke, and no one ever heard him with a curse or foul word on his mouth. Poor old Kid! You have no idea how I miss him. We were in different sections, but we never let very long go by without looking each other up and passing on the latest news from home. He passed the last one to see him in the communications trench and even there, with the shells dropping around like snowflakes in a blizzard, he cracked a joke as he passed. Now Dad, I want you to go down to Mr. Stewart and tell him what you think is best, and remember that there is always a chance he is a prisoner. (Fritz got about 60 prisoners out of the mess.) Tell him that I can't bear to write to him about it, but if there is anything he wants to know I'll be pleased to look after it for him. Privately, I rather am of the opinion that Chet is out for good. Just before I went on leave we were talking about his O.C. He remarked then that Mr. Neal had all the nerve in the world but for all that, he was too foolish with it. I warned him then that no matter what the officer did, to keep his own head. He laughed and remarked that he guessed he could follow any place the Officer would lead. His Officer is gone, so can't help, but be of the opinion that Chet is gone. I know for a fact that if the Officer started anything Chet wouldn't leave him to finish himself. He was too good a soldier and much of a man. On second thought, Daddy mine, I think you should show this part of this letter to the Rev. McIntyre and let him speak to Mr. Stewart. Not that I think he could do it better than you, but coming from him it will be much better, but Dad, please tell Mr. Stewart that I most certainly sympathise with him and the rest of the family with all my heart and will do all in my power to find out for certain one way or the other.

Oh Dad, you have no idea how I miss them all. At times I get so very, very down heartened that I wish I had gone with them. Just one more word before I finish about Chet and it's this. I'd give anything I possess to be able to feel that when I go I'd leave as big a vacant place in the hearts of all my comrades. Pass on my condolences to Annie. But at that, Chet was more to me than to her. To me Chet has been ever since we enlisted, a pattern of what I'd like to be and an inspiration.

As for Rex Tucker and Alan Bowie, they were both killed. Rex was shot in the head and died in a few minutes. He died with a bomb in his hand, and game to the last; he tried to throw it. His last words just after he was hit were, "Oh Mother, Oh Mother". I can't talk about it anymore dear folks of mine. I'll have to change the subject, but don't forget to show this to the Rev. McIntyre and please don't let the content of this go any further than necessary because – well I guess you'll understand.

I am going to tell you about my leave but I can't in this. Will write later and tell you all about it. Saw Waldo and all the other boys and stayed with them until they left for France. I am going to try and have Waldo transferred to us. Must close now, so long

As ever,
Your loving son and Brother, Roy

Somehow life continues here with normal activities. The Automobile Club with 100 cars did their first run

of the season. Arch was happy. I tease him he was one of the 99 (sheep)who strayed and only 1 got lost and was found. We took the girls and Geordie who got to swim and go boating. We left before the dancing started. Arch loves the water. Later there was a huge parade of 2,000 autos, many from out of town.

While I follow the local happenings and, of course, war news, I forget there Is life going on in other places in Saskatchewan. For the first half of the year, 2,571 new homesteads were started in the province. The total for all of Western Canada was 6,895, a decrease from the same period a year ago. 70% are English speaking. Arch has hired two new salesmen to go on the road!

50 tons of railroad steel arrived from Edmonton. It is to be laid for streetcar tracks over the new 25th Street bridge.

July 1916

It is such a tragedy when the total numbers of Canadian casualties for the month are published. July's list filled 22 pages – row after row of closely packed tiny print. The Returned Veterans still cling to their horrible experiences. They are making replica trenches at the fairgrounds. I doubt if they will add mud, latrines, rats and other vermin. I wonder why this need to build these trenches.

I had a rather fine experience on Tuesday. I have been trying to go for a walk each afternoon. I went down Lansdowne, crossed 8th Street and at the corner of 6th Street, I planned to walk east on 6th Street to Broadway and then home. However, there was a lady out in her front yard with the sweetest little girl. She told me her name was Bertha and she is five years old. The lady and I chatted and both expressed we had seen one another somewhere. I suggested maybe it was at Westminster Church, but the go to 3rd Avenue Methodist. Such a friendly lady, she asked me to come the next day for tea.

I went to tea. They are Mr. and Mrs. E. Watson. He is a contractor, and my brother Jim knows him. Mrs. Watson had invited a neighbour, Mrs. Gordon. As we chatted, we discovered an interesting connection. The Gordons are related to the Stewarts who own the drugstore on Broadway. Arch is a close friend of Mr. Stewart and we always have a little joke. He calls me his long lost cousin, as my name was also Stewart. Everyone always seems to find a connection to someone else.

So I had two enjoyable afternoons. I didn't think about the war for even one moment. This is how the world should be!

September 1916

Arnold Anderson sent a letter dated August 24th to his Dad in Saskatoon. He titled it "Life in the Trenches". He was in charge of the same men he had in Saskatoon. He reported 6 hours of sleep in 24 hours. They stayed in trenches for two days. He was trying to be humorous when he said Canadians are at "home" as they attract a better quality of mosquitoes because the men tasted good, "dirty as a pet coon". He told how they squished the bugs, and rats could be as big as weasels.

Both boys are remiss in keeping in touch from Camp Hughes in Manitoba. Willie sent a post card of Camp Hughes. I don't think the true horror of the actual war has sunk into them. They both sound excited. They are in the best physical shape in their lives. They march miles each day, some with full gear. Bill commented now he knows why men with flat feet are rejected. They are learning how to take apart their rifles and how to read maps, but the most important lesson is to follow orders without any questions! They can't tell us when, but they will likely be in England before year's end and so their letters will eventually come from England. I will try not to worry as their future is in the hands of "The Higher Power".

October 1916

October continued with more pages of casualties. Some we knew George Wells of 544 4th Avenue North, F. Woodcock, Superintendent of Street Railways and Charles Warner, Secretary-Treasurer of Boy Scouts. He was also Treasurer of St. James Social Club. Hugh knew him through Boy Scouts/

December 1916

The month of December rolled by wrapped in sadness and loss. Then Scarlet Fever broke out in several spots. 11 had to be hospitalized.

Charles Ross, 19, of Moose Jaw and a member of the 128th Battalion, made a sale to the government for the unheard of total of 1 million Dollars. He worked for 4 years to get the patent for his device to transmit Electrical Energy by wireless. It can generate a current of 3,200 volts, transmitting 4 thousand miles. It was obtaining the patent that made him a millionaire.

On December 23rd, Westminster Sunday School held its Annual Christmas Tree. The crowded hall raised

$50 for the Belgian Relief Fund. Jim was involved as a leader and teacher. Mr. Cameron was Chairman. Of course, the programme started with choruses and motion songs by the Primary Class. Helen Hay sang a patriotic solo called "I want my Daddy". The Chinese did a chorus and Dr. Dix gave an address (not a real sermon!). Jim asked Geordie to do a recitation called "Fun to Scrap the Plan". He did a fine job. Barbara Gold and Woodburn McCallum did a recitation. Of course, they had drills, and a bell chorus.

What a wonderful evening, normal enjoyment as in days of yore. And then we realize how many are missing. Is that called "bitter-sweet"?

No word yet from Hugh or Bill.

1917

January 1917

Our Christmas of 1916 was too quiet without the boys. Helen and Nan said we should buy each brother a new book, wrap it and put it under our Christmas tree. The books will remain unopened until they are home.

I prepared all our favourite dishes and yet nothing tasted quite right. We have Jim and Geordie new watches and the girls got new bracelets.. Luckily Nan loves gold colour and silver is Helen's passion. As always, Arch picked out a lovely new brooch for me. We spent more time at various church services.

At last! Word from the boys! Hugh was the first to leave Camp Hughes and arrived in England on November 1, 1916. Willie finally reported with a short note to say he arrived safely on November 11. Rough seas and fears of torpedoes mad the voyage not like a holiday excursion. They both said they are relatively safe as they will be in England for further courses before they go to France or Belgium. We will have to learn more patience as they are not able to write on a regular basis.

January 12, 1917

The Phoenix announced Recruit Standards have changed. The required height is now 4' 11". Also, more men with flat feet will be accepted. I realized the significance as Willie had commented that endless marching was necessary. Also, I can't believe what I am reading – in most cases, a soldier needs sight in only one eye. One must read D-200 at 20' with the right eye, no glasses, and not less than D-80 without glasses.

The children seem to be doing well at school. Nan and Jim are at Nutana. All of them have friends and are hardly ever home, so it seems to me. Jim is faithful to make sure chores are done. He is "training" Geordie – after all, he is past twelve! It is time! I never have to worry about wood or snow shovelled. It is lonely – I wish Arch could stay home more.

February 1917

It is the end of February. I have not recorded much all month. Local news seems trivial. All we have received is a brief letter from each boy. They really tell us nothing and then we checked the dates they wrote and then go right back to imagine that they are already dead. Bill is fighting in Belgium and Hugh in France.

At the last meeting of the United Commercial Travellers, Arch was elected to sit on the Grand Council. This brought Arch out of him doom and gloom. He was given a silver watch fob in the shape of a club bag. The inscription is UTC Grand Council. He plans to give it to Bill when he gets home.

The Nutana Collegiate budget was printed in the newspaper. Five itemized sources of revenue were listed. Receipts totalled over $56,000. The biggest expenditure was $32,000 for teachers. Fuel was only about $2,000 for the year. Arch thinks that is quite good. The heating system, installed at the beginning, proves to be a good investment. The Caretaker and supplies were over $3,000. They certainly did not spend much money on the library and reference books – only $59! W. Bate is the Secretary Treasurer and is very good.

WORLD WAR 1 PHOTO OF GROUP- WILLIAM MUNRO, FRONT ROW, EXTREME RIGHT. C1917

Bill Munro (Front Row, Extreme Right) in Europe with the soldiers in his unit.

April 1917

April begins! I have a bad feeling. I think as spring comes, the fighting overseas will increase. Both boys report that they are not getting many letters, so some must be getting lost.

May 1917

I will always remember May 1917. Arch had brought home two boxes of chocolates. One was Moir's and the other Melba Chocolates. We were having fun, tasting and voting on our favourites. It had been a long time since we were laughing and shouting over one another. I had just cast my vote for Melba's apricot jelly when we were interrupted by a wire from Donald and Alice in North Battleford. Young Jack had been killed on April 29th. Sadness overwhelms us all. I don't think I can eat another apricot jelly chocolate. The soft centre now makes me think of congealed blood.

Jack's death was the lone Saskatoon casualty listed in the May 5th paper. Our Jim is devastated as he and Jack were the same age. Jim could have enlisted on this 18th birthday, but I know he knows we can't bear another son at war. It's true – we very much need him to be safe with us.

I was too sad to record anything for a while, but now I want to express one of my most difficult moments in my life. I was the cause of immense, unforgettable pain to Nan and Helen. I seek forgiveness from God daily.

I didn't realize how shattered my nerves were after Jack's death. One morning, while Arch was away, the girls were bickering and arguing over who got to wear a shared sweater. All of a sudden, I found myself sobbing and I screamed at the girls, "How can you be so terrible when your brothers could be dead?" I will never forget the look on their faces. They clung to each other as if one would collapse if the other didn't hold on.

We were at a total impasse. I could not take back my cruel words. Jim, bless him forever, was the calm voice that saved us all from destruction. Jim addressed me, and in the kindest voice sad, "Mother, do you know the girls are hurting as much as you are? We are all trying so hard to carry on as normal, but our lives are not normal right now. You are not carrying this all by yourself, no should any of us try to shoulder our pain alone." He then asked Nan, who seemed a little calmer, "What is your biggest hurt and how can we help you?" Through her sniffles, Nan said she was surprised herself about what she missed the most. She said she missed Willie, as they used to sit in the big chair and read together when she was younger. "Now I try to read alone, but it hurts so much that it might never happen again." Jim asked her if it would help if he sat and read with her. Nan half smiled through her tears and replied, "You can't read as well as Willie, but if you had a candy or two in your pocket, like Willie did, it would help me!"

It took him a little longer to find out Helen's biggest hurt. I was shocked at her answer. "I can't start my day with our prayers at breakfast. I need to start the day without stirring the ache in my heart. I need to be happy and it seems like I'm just begging God to spare my brothers and He didn't spare Jack!" Once again Jim wisely said, "You should skip morning prayers and pray at night and thank God for giving you joy." Helen hesitated, then looked up timidly at me and asked if that would be okay. Both girls came over and we all hugged. Then Jim asked me the dreaded question, "What hurts you the most?" I could not identify a single hurt that was the deepest, so I found myself expressing my worries about their father. I said, "Your father is such a good man, and he has sacrificed so much by being away from home to give a good life." And so the discussion turned to how we could support Archie.

We all agreed that their father hides his emotions and survives by trying to carry his burden alone. Nan spoke up and said her father used to take her on walks. He would tell her little stories about his childhood, about what they saw on their walks, or he would make up silly songs. She said she hadn't spent much time with him lately, so she decided she would take him on walks on the weekends and share her stories. Helen offered that as she knew morning prayers were important to him, she would come to the table when he was home.

The girls calmed down and Jim gave me another look that was filled with love and concern, yet his look let me know that he knew I had sidestepped his first question. I then knew my look was a reflection of his deep hurt. His way of coping was to watch over and protect us, just like the boys did.

Not all sadness and death have to happen overseas. J.F. Cairns' son Jack drowned in Pike Lake when his canoe capsized. He was only 15. Mr. Cairns has been a major force in the growth and richness of life in Saskatoon. Other earlier settlers make good sums of money here and then left. Cairns built a fine department store, and he did make lots of money, but he was always supporting and giving back to the community. I pray for them, too.

June 30th, 1917

A lot has happened the last half of June.

The Exhibition was being used for barracks, but all the bunks, mess and fixtures were taken out and stored for a week so the Exhibition could be held as usual.

On June 18th, they opened the Home for Returned Soldiers. The I.O.D.E. held a linen shower and lots of bedding was donated. The afternoon tea netted $71.00. All four upstairs bedrooms are filled.

One of the strangest happenings was when Physics Professor W. S. Fyfe, an electrical engineer predicts a watch-sized telephone, operated by wireless electricity, will be in tablets the size of a pack of chewing gum. His Tele-pestograph will be able to tell what someone else is doing all the time.

On June 29th, a picnic was planned by the Great War Veterans. They had music and dancing and the Returned Soldier's Band played. It felt as if summer had returned and so many children went to see Jim Patterson's Trained Wild Animal Show. They had 300 horses and many other animals.

Of course, daily reports of casualties continue. Some Saskatoon names are Stanley Creighton, William Black, Charlie Gallagher, Alford La Tour and Gordon O'Leary as well as George Youmans and John Nelson who were chums for years. I pray that all were believers in God.

July 1917

The circus arrived by train at 5 am on July 7th. They put on a parade at 11 am. There were three marching bands. They put on an afternoon and an evening show.

Geordie loved it the most. He wants a horse so badly as he just barely remembers our horse in Morden.

The paper reported there are 30,084 autos registered in the province.

Various organizations are always sending parcels overseas. Westminster Church works hard to send parcels to our lads. They have committed to send cigarettes – a strange thing for a church to be doing – but that is what the boys want and need. I have been getting more involved with this effort and it has been good for me.

August 1917

At the beginning of August, Arch planned something special for our family and the North Battleford Munros. I was trying to think of some wat of spending time with Alice. Arch rented a shack at Meota for a week. We drove up to N. B. very early Sunday morning. We arrived just in time to go straight to Church. After church and a light lunch, we left for the lake in two cars. We took our four children and Donald and Alice had Helen, 21, and George, 23, who was home from university. Tassie, 26, is in Vancouver studying to be a nurse.

On Monday morning, Arch, Donald, George, Jim and Geordie Mack left for our farm at Marsden. The brothers needed time alone and did lots or remembering their youth at Finch, Ontario. Our Geordie Mack loved their stories and he formed a bond with his older cousin George, who was very kind to a young boy who was missing his older brothers.

Alice, the two Helens, Nan and I stayed on alone. Their cousin Helen was splendid with Nan, 17 and our Helen, 15. They spent most of the day swimming and going exploring. Alice and I took a splash every afternoon and just were quiet together.

Arch pulled in for us about noon on Thursday. We had a bonfire Thursday night, all 10 of us. We started for home Friday morning. Donald was in such good spirits he wanted to stay on. He planned to write his Sunday sermon by the water. He said, "No war, no killing, no trials, just the simple Love of God and His gifts of nature." Alice said his sermon helped a lot of the church folk there. They drove to N. B. on Saturday afternoon.

There was a little advertisement in the paper for Dr. Chase's Ointment. They started by saying thoughtful mothers send a little time to their warrior sons. They promoted their product as good for minor skin irritations and even piles. I cut two copies and sent one to each boy with a little tin of Dr. Chase's. Both boys responded and they had a good chuckle and so did we. Geordie took it too far and in school said both his brothers had terrible piles.

October 1917

On October 9, death came knocking close to home – in fact, right next door at 420. Our neighbour James Coulter died suddenly from a heart attack. He was 53 years old, the same age as Arch! James had been in the city since 1903, but they moved next door in 1911. They bought the house from Richard Raul. James was a contractor. I hurried and made sandwiches and took them across in the morning in case they needed them before the funeral. Several ladies on our block sent baking. Arch was away so Nan and I paid our respects. I was pleased when Nan graciously helped the two Coulter girls serve.

November 1917

Often weeks go by with no news, but we faithfully write a letter to each boy every Sunday evening. It is strange, but every Monday morning that I walk over to the Post Office to mail them, I gain a sense of purpose again. Arch always finds a topic other than the war in hopes that it helps them be connected to us. He made the rule that our letters cannot start with "How are you?" He says they will tell us in their own way and the question might force them to tell a lie. Also, by the time we get an answer, that question would have a different answer. Arch tries to include a report about the Kirk, or local news, or stories about his life on the road. I secretly chuckle as he always wants to conclude each letter "We are all fine". Often we are not!

Many of our friends or even acquaintances are careful to pass on any information they might receive in one of their son's letters. So it was that Cliff McConnell mentioned in his letter to his folks that they had heard Hugh had been wounded. They came right across to share and ask if we had heard anything. Immediately Arch sent a telegram via Canadian Pacific Railway Company to the Director of Records in Ottawa.

The next day, on November 10th, we got a reply that no further information regarding Pt. Hugh Archie

Munro. It said as soon as they receive the present condition and nature of his wounds, they will pass it on.

We had no word from either lad for quite a while.

On November 14th, 1917, we got a telegram from the Red Cross Society and we assumed it was information about Hugh. It was about Bill.

CANADIAN RED CROSS SOCIETY

Dear Madame,

I beg to inform you that Private W. M. Munro 46th Battalion Canadians, No. 910871 is now at Kitchener's War Hospital, Brighton, England.

He came here from France on Dec. 9th having been in hospital in France. He was wounded on Nov. 28th by gunshot on his chest rather severely.

We will shortly have a fuller report for you, he was very cheerful when he arrived. Rest assured he will receive the best of care, he is in a splendid hospital.

Yours truly,
Cloustance H Scott

We had no further word about either boy. Then, on December 1st, we received Bill's letter dated November 11, 1917

Blighty Nov. 11/17

Dear Dad. I did not mail this letter in France as envelopes were scarce. On account of artery cut I am not allowed to move much but am very comfortable and my appetite and my "embonpoint"? I am called Bulgy Algy by a dear Scotch nurse. My unshaven face suggested Teddy Bear to a student nurse who was also very good.

You will likely have heard of our stunt on the 26th. We went over in the morning after living in shell holes for four days. The weather was rotten. Rain every night. We had touch luck when we went over. I had to take charge of an M. G. although I had never fired one before. It was so dirty that it would only fire one shot at a time. I had lots of fun sniping until about 3 o'clock when it became certain that we were going to be under attack heavily. I took the M. G. to the dug out and took it to pieces and cleaned it and just finished when I had to get busy. Even then the gun would now and then fail to completely extract and I had to keep a screw driver handy to pull out the cartridge. After a time it got too hot and we were in danger of being flanked from the left and cut off. An officer ordered us to fall back. We'll be here two months. Although it is not the best time it seems full of promise. Many have been wounded.

Billy

Jim and Arch poured over Bill's letter. They figured the first telegram said he had chest wounds when really it was much worse. A few words in a letter somehow tells so much.

December 1917

Finally, just before Christmas, we received Hugh's letter dated December 13, 1917.

Foye House
Leigh Woods
Bristol, Dec 13/17

My Dear Mother

Just a note to say Hello, had a letter from Harold Blair this Morning he has had his leave + is back again. He sent me the card I am sending you.

Had a card from Fred Struthers yesterday he was in London on leave + going to Edinburgh that night. I expect to be transferred to a Canadian Hospital soon but address the same Foy House + it will be forwarded to me. I will be sorry to leave this place it is so nice and such nice nurses.

Saw by the Daily Mail this morning the Lieut. C. McConnell has died a prisoner in German hands. I was sorry to hear it as it must be Cliff as it said Sask Regt.

I had some lovely Snaps from Cora Thompson Sunday taken in Banff where she spent her summer holiday.

Well no new is good news so I'll ring off for now. Had a letter from Bill + he is alright. Heaps of love to everyone.

As ever

Hugh

As usual, Hugh does not even mention what his wounds are, but he puts the return address as Bristol, England. I think one of his previous letters did not reach us.

Even though Hugh is in hospital, he writes a newsy cheery letter. I contacted all the people he mentioned. I wanted them to know their children had sent letters to Hugh and to thank their own children for writing. First I called Harold Blair's father. They live at 212 9th Street. They were pleased. Cora Thompson's father is also a traveller. Arch sees him quite often. They live at 511 9th Street. Cora was so thoughtful to send Hugh pictures of Banff. I did not reach Fred Struthers' family. The very hard one is the death of our dear neighbour boy Cliff McConnell. They were notified earlier in December. What heartache for them. A wonderful light was snuffed out and in such a cruel manner.

Like Bill and John D., Cliff and his brother Doug planned to be lawyers. Imagine – all of them lived on the 400 block of 9th Street.

1918

January 1918

The year of our Lord, 1918 anno domini arrived.

We cancelled Christmas! I baked very little, only the favourites of each lad. Willie loved my tiny mincemeat tarts. He called them "two biters" and then would open his mouth wide and pop in a whole tart. Then, after chewing, he would always say "Oops, just a one biter!" How I wish I could see him do that again. Not many were eaten and those that were, eaten without fanfare.

Hugh loves shortbread, so I made quite a bit, but I took most of it to the Christmas bake sale at the Church.

When people heard both boys were wounded, letters of concern and prayers flowed from many of our brothers and sisters, cousins and friends. The letters helped some, but some unintentionally hurt. As "comforting" comments were offered, such as "Hugh <u>was</u> such a nice guy" or "Bill <u>was</u> always an instigator of fun", instead of comforting, they made us consider that the boys may never be home. I just noticed I did the same – "Bill loved tarts" and "Hugh <u>loved</u> shortbread". I never want to hear the past tense used about soldiers.

We all went to church and prayed not only for our boys, but for so many that are lost or injured. Helen was very upset and sat with her eyes dripping tears and her head bowed. I know she still feels guilty about not wanting to pray every morning.

The first great news was a letter from Bill dated December 4, 1917.

Dec.4.1917

Dear Dad: Here I am looking like someone who had attempted suicide! Am feeling fine and am enjoying 24 hours rest and four meals a day. Am half mad with homesickness and lonesomeness and am very anxious about Hugh. But you will have heard from him before you get this. The mail has not started to come yet but hope it will soon and I will get much of it. I know I have not written as much as you would like, **but I have really done my best**.

Winter is here and you can have it. I am glad to miss it. <u>Gee</u>, I wish I was at home.

❧❧

Then on January 10th, a second letter arrived, this one from Hugh.

❧❧

Sunday
Dec. 16-17

Dear Mother,

Just a note to say Hello I am still at Faye House + don't know when I will move. I had my fortune told last night + they said four days. My nurse would like me to be here for Xmas but I don't think I will be.

She is very nice. It seems very funny for her to be sweeping and dusting walls, dressing heads + carrying meals at all hours of the day. She is a rich married lady with a cook + six servants who do her work at home + she does the work here.

I have moved today into a different ward and there are only four of us here. It is a very nice ward.

I had a letter from J.C. Passmore, the man John Gorien told to look after me in the 196th. I don't know if you remember him. He is being invalided home to S'toon and will call + see you. He is a very nice fellow, an Englishman.

I have had no mail for a week and it was old mail then. A lot of fellows are going home for Xmas out of Hospital and it is very nice for them to have homes so near. It is very lonesome at Xmas with nobody that you know.

Tell the kids to write often + I will try to answer. I wrote Grannie last week. I had a letter from her a week ago.

Well I must say So short for now. I haven't heard from Bill for a couple of days but he is OK.

With love
Hugh
Foye House Leigh Woods, Bristol

With renewed vigor, we all wrote lots of letters in hopes that some would reach them.

On January 26th, we received a letter from the Department of Militia and Defence

Department of Militia and Defence

OTTAWA,_____January 20th, 1918

From:-

The Adjutant-General,
Canadian Militia

To:-

A. Munro Esq.,
422 Ninth St.,
Saskatoon, Sask.

910871 Private William McKeith Munro,
Canadian Expeditionary Force.

Sir:-

I have the honour to state that information has been received, by mail, from England, to the effect that the marginally noted soldier, who has been suffering from a gunshot wound in the neck, penetrating the jugular vein, was transferred from Kitchener's Military Hospital, Brighton, England, to Military Convalescent Hospital, Woodcote Park, Epsom, England, on December 22, 1917

2.   Any further information received will be communicated to you without delay.

I have the honour to be
Sir,
Your obedient servant,
Frank Beard
Director of Records
ESC   *for a/Adjutant-General.*

However, Bill's letter had reached us about his cut artery, so we did know, but the official report came as a shock. We learned he had been wounded at Passchendaele. From all reports, it was a terrible fight. Someone saved his life! We were shocked how many times they moved him. On November 8th he was transferred from étaples, France to #6 British Hospital. Then on November 14th, he was finally moved to Kitchener's Military Hospital in Brighton and on November 17th to Bramshott. He was there until December 22nd when he was finally moved to the Military Convalescent Hospital in Woodcote Park.

There is a serious coal shortage. One suggestion is to shut down the playhouses in Canada for 3 days a week.

On January 31st, I could not believe my eyes. J. F. Cairns put up a blood stained flag from Flanders Fields in the store window. Every mother will imagine it is her son's blood. It is hard to read the newspapers. Daily and monthly lists are printed of Canadian casualties. Often there are 24 pages of names in very fine print. I seem to get irritated when bits of news, not about the war, are printed. Example – the Province has issued 5,000 auto licences, 1,500 more than last year. Or – a new force water main to Nutana was finally completed after 3 years at the cost of $70,000. Who really cares!

February 1918

On February 2nd, 74 train cars of coal arrived on CNR and another 24 cars will arrive by CPR. Arch is always careful to have a good supply on hand, but we have tried to cut back. People's Fuel and Suppl Co. had a good advertisement in the Daily Star:

"If you are putting in a good supply of coal, do so before your plant your garden. Order Red Deer Coal and get it before the ground gets too soft."

March 1918

I had planned a fun outing for Arch and myself. Imagine! Harry Lauder was to come here on March 4th. He calls it his "Farewell American Tour". It was to be at the 3rd Avenue Methodist Church. I bought the most expensive tickets - $3. Guess what! No Harry Lauder, but we were gifted with the worst snowstorm in years.

The Quakers hockey team was to play in Winnipeg, but the train got only to Clavet. G. G. Elliott rescued passengers with one sleigh pulled by four horses and two other sleighs pulled by two horses each. Luckily Arch had stayed in the city. All we could do was put on our Harry Lauder record and sing along!

An interesting report about the Chinese community was in the Daily Star. Generally the Chinese do not have a good reputation. Their cafes were often involved in the drug trade. A year ago, a Chinese Y. M. C. A. was started. There are about 200 Chinese men in the city and over 50 are members. It is good to see some Chinese men holding key positions. Mark Wah is president and the Vice-President is Mah Kie. There is also a Chines Nationalist League. Many Chinese belong. I think they are on the right track. They are trying to improve how citizens view them. They are wearing Canadian clothes, learning to speak English and learning Canadian political ideals.

Jim was so excited when he got his own letter from Hugh. Usually a shortage of paper and stamps make it so that letters have to be shared by the family.

France
March 12-18

Dear Jim

Well, don't you consider it your solemn duty to write your warrior brother who is doing his warrioring a long way from the front line by a very peaceful little running brook.

There is absolutely nothing to say except that the weather is fine and will continue to be so until it rains I expect.

How are the youngsters behaving themselves. I hope none of them have thrown you out yet.

How do you manage to exist without the Moes and Mildreds etc. it must be lonesome of course I have forgotten that there are such things as girls but then I'm very old you know.

By the way seeing you're earning $96 per month you're a friend worth writing to. Just by way of suggestion you know if ever you want to send any of your soldier friends in France a present I don't mean myself of course, why I think a box of chocolates is very much appreciated by the troops. That's not a hint though to read it might give one that impression.

I wrote to Bill whose nick name is Towser, yesterday. I hope to hear from him soon. Well Jim I must say bonjour for now – will write again soon. Drop me a line when you have time.

As ever
Hugh

46 BN Canadian BEF
France

An order was issued from Ottawa, increasing the scope of the Military Service Act. They want to call for a thousand more men, so all 19 year old males and childless widowers will be conscripted.

May 1918

Arch's brother Peter James (P. J.) and Pearl did have their third child, James Munro. The two girls, Kathleen and Jean, are three and four. We went on Sunday see wee James and take gifts for all the children. They still live on the West side, so we don't go there very often.

I was pleased to get two letters from Hugh in one envelope.

France
April 27-18

My Dear Mother

It is dark and nearly time for bed so I am just dropping a note. Have been digging all day and am rather tired.

No mail has come here for me yet but I will likely have some soon.

I occasionally meet fellows I know but none of the old section as yet. I guess they must be in the line.

Well lights are out + I can't see what I am writing so I better close for now.

Best Love to all

As ever
Hugh
46 BN Canadians
B. E. F. France

April 28-18

Dear Mother:-

I find I have not posted the last letter I wrote so will put in a few more lines. I was very glad today to get three letters from home. It had seemed quite a while between mails though it was not two weeks. I guess it was because we have been moving around so much the time has seemed long.

Congrats to the other Munros – I guess they would be glad to have a boy by way of a change.

So Jack & Rhoda are still going strong eh? I have not heard from him for a while but Ruth told me they had started writing to each other again.

I saw Bill the night I left Bramshott he was on guard at the segregation Camp.

I owe a lot of letters but don't know when I will settle down to answer them. Tell Jim I got his & will write him again soon. So Nan hears from Joe eh? I guess she will miss him but tell her I thinks she's very fickle to be going out with another boy the same day as she saw Joe away ha ha-

Well I must close now have not had Dad's letter yet but will write him soon. It is raining as usual I think that after this month it will clear up.

Best love to Dad, Mother the <u>kids</u>

As ever
Hugh
46 BN BEF
France

On May 7th, the news of the death of Fred Struthers was reported. He was not wounded but died of pneumonia in France. Gone is another mate of the boys. How quickly they are gone. In Hugh's letter written last December, he mentions he had a card from Fred. He was in London on leave and on his way to Edinburgh.

I feel so much calmer now after I heard from Bill and then we got news of Hugh by way of a letter sent from Colonsay, by Hugh's friend Cliff Whyte.

How do you like the work in the bank. I'm afraid I wouldn't be much good for that job. Do you remember my chief failing was Math. Do you know I am actually intending to go to the Farm when I go home? It requires quite a stretch of imagination to think of me as a farmer but you remember Jack

Gower. He didn't know any more about it than I do and he is doing it.

You probably know that Gordon Cummings and Aubrey Bate and Harold Brown are all back in Saskatoon again. Aubrey seemingly has taken to flights of oratory since he returned. I hear that he was to give a spiel in Third Ave. Methodist Church one afternoon. I wish I could have been there to hear it.

Where is your brother who enlisted? Has he got to France yet?

It is two months since I came back and we have had a dandy time. We are bivouacked in a field 50,000 miles from anywhere – we can't even hear the guns. It is a very pleasant way to spend the summer but I don't know how long it will last. Not very much longer, I guess.

Sincerely, your old pal, Hugh

June 1918

On a happy note, I encountered Mrs. Freeman. I used to go to her restaurant on Broadway for an afternoon cup of tie and a piece of her delicious pie. The Alex-ander Freemans did not have any children, but in the summer of 1915, they adopted the sweetest baby girl named Verna. Her mother and her mother's best friend, Dr. McConnell's wife, Alma, were walking along Broadway with Verna between them. What a beautiful child! They asked me to join them for tea at the Broadway Café. Both women did not realize how much this meant to me. I forgot about wars and tribulations. I had almost forgotten the feeling of joy and pride being a mother to my two little girls.

I was on my way home and decided to walk along Twelfth Street to Eastlake. I looked up and say young George trotting along. He was coming from the wrong direction. Now once in a while Willie would skip school for the afternoon, take his satchel with and apple and a book inside and hike along the riverbank, find his favourite tree, climb it and read his book. Some teachers at the high school knew about these adventures – usually in June or September. But they closed their eyes to it, because he was just enjoying nature and reading. George had a guilty look on his face and I just knew he had skipped school. Before I could start a lecture, Geordie confessed he remembered how Willie used to skip school and Geordie decided he would try it himself.

He hiked a while, but that does not come naturally to him. He had difficulty finding the right tree as they were too spindly or too tall. He finally struggled up a tree, ripping his trousers. He tried to read, but was afraid he would fall out of the tree.

As he explained about his adventure, he told me how he felt so close to his oldest brother. Somehow this adventure had turned more into a pilgrimage. He said it was almost as if Willie was right there, admonishing him to grow up, establish some goals for himself and push himself to do more.

His seriousness impacted me and I said he should not consider it a frivolous afternoon, but a very important afternoon. I suggested whereas Willie did his best thinking in a tree, that he should find a spot, such as in a manicured park and lie on the grass.

On June 19th there was a huge hailstorm. It lasted a solid 9 minutes. It was more severe at the University. 3,000 windows were blown out. The estimated cost to repair is $20,000. The storm seemed worse along the river. St. John's had about $1,000 damage. At Knox, the memorial windows were damaged. We had only one gable window broken. Also, at Campbell &

Cooper on 20th Street, thieves entered through broken windows and stole rifles and ammo.

Bikes and motorcycles have had a speed limit in the city enacted – 15 miles per hour.

At the end of June, we received this letter dated June 11th, 1918. After sharing it, Geordie and I just looked at one another. Geordie was sure June 11 was the day he went for a walk to read by the riverbank.

FRANCE, JUNE 11, 1918

Dear Dad: This morning I went for a short route march which enabled me to enjoy a dinner of beef and stewed raisins. This afternoon I am spending in the woods, resting. The day is perfect and the quiet natural surroundings and the creaminess of my pipe, which is more than ordinarily well behaved, make me the rival of the author of "Adventures in Contentment". Although I have had no mail for some time I know it is piling up somewhere and that I will have a great time when I get it.

I am so lazy that I can hardly write but I think it is a useful laziness. Haven't felt so sane for a long time. Of course it would be much more pleasant if I could babble this to you here, but this is next best. My mood being introspective, I am useless as a source of information but because so, I am, Your friend, Billy

July 1918

Exhibition time again – July 13th – 20th.

Eaton's had a large tent at the Exhibition. Also Walter's Cycle Co. had a nice display. Thousands of citizens and visitors were at the Travellers' Day parade. It was led by the band of Johnny Jones.

Arch lives for this. I made him a new clown suit. In spite of the ware, there were many decorated floats. Gate receipts were over $19,000 and the grandstand brought in over $9,000. Concessions earned $8 - $9 thousand and about $15,000 was paid out in prizes. 109,635 people rode the street cars during the week.

So far the summer has been very busy. Willie's 23rd birthday was July 2nd. We sent him a special parcel and everyone wrote a letter. Jim finished up at Nutana passing the Matriculation/Teacher course. We planned a special birthday. I made a cake and nan decorated it.

The next evening we invited several of his chums for the evening. When word got out, a few of Willie's and Hugh's friends heard about it and asked to come. In the past the boys would play card games or charades, but they seemed more interested in just visiting. All their boyhoods are over and they are serious young men. They had a great singsong and Jim gave a serious and moving speech. Arch was thrilled to be included. He said Jim's speech could easily be considered a fine sermon.

The girls and I sat on the top stair and listened. Geordie was the server. An evening to remember!

France
June 25-18

My Dear Mother

Just received your letter written on May 13 and also two from Jim. I was very glad to get them too. Did you ever send the pictures of you and Dad. I never got them. I wish you would send one if you haven't done so yet

I was over to see the fellows at the Battalion on Sunday and saw a great many old friends. I did not see Mr. Blair as he had a horse and was away for a ride somewhere.

I don't expect to be going back to them for a while anyway as I am now with the Canadian Corps Survey Section — not Civil Engineers. They do observation work for the Corps. It ought to be very interesting work. I don't know when we will be going up the line. At present we are having instruction.

We are near a good town and have a good time.

I have not got the parcels you sent yet but will likely get them soon there is a Canadian mail in now.

I had a peach of a letter from Miss Bennett last week it had lots of Collegiate news in it. I also had one from Lu, she is working in San Francisco and having a peach of a time in the tender care of her Uncle Mart or else he's in her tender care. I don't know which one is most capable of chaperonage or which needs it more. Her letter was full of fun and I had a great laugh. I have not heard from Jack Gonier for some time but I guess he is very busy with farm work, so I'll drop him a line soon.

Well I must say so long for now. I did not see Billy before I left the last place. I guess he'll be there by now.

Best love to dad, yourself and "The dear little children" ha ha

I bet that will make them rave.

As ever
Hugh

I'll put my address on the back
#911004 HAM
Canadian Corps Survey Section
Observers B.E.F. France

On the 15th, this short letter arrived from Bill.

I have nothing to report.

Am writing to Uncle Donald tonight Guess this will hit you about my birthday when I will be what is it? 23? Gee but I'm getting old. You never mention very much about your own wee troubles and I think I should Know some of 'em. Tell you enough of mine don't I.

Well this letter writing is a pretty poor thing when one can't tell what little they could and going to quit "covering the Page".

We think Bill and Jim are our deep thinkers. Bill can express so much in just a few written words. Jim expresses himself better verbally.

Mother arrived and she proudly carried this letter from Hugh with her

France
June 25-18

Dear Grannie

Many thanks for the letter I received the other night. Was glad to hear that you are keeping well, Grannie and hope you have a good trip west this summer.

I wish I could be in Saskatoon when you are there. Had a letter from Mother last night and she said she was getting lonesome to see you again, it is pretty quiet for her with the three boys away from home. I hope it will not be long 'til we are all back again.

The weather has been fine lately and we have had a good time.

Tass has an Overland now and seems to be enjoying things very much. Her dad must be making lots of money to be buying so many cars these days.

The war was looking pretty dull for a while but is getting better the last couple of weeks. The Italians have given the Austrians quite a blow.

Hope all the Wpg. Folks are well. Will write again soon.

Best love to all
As ever
Hugh

911004 Pte. H. A. Munro
Observers
Canadian Corps Survey Sect. B. E. F.
France

France
July 17-18

Dear Mother and Dad

I forget whether it is today or yesterday that the congratulations were due but will send them along anyway and wish you many more anniversaries.

Thanks very much for the parcel I received a couple of days ago. The fellows laughed when the pack of cards + the testament came out together. It was on a Sunday so we tossed for which we should use first + played a game of 500.

We have moved now + are getting ready to get to work again after our rest. Are in a very nice place.

Had a note from Billie the other day he has not yet joined the Batt. + may not do so for a while. He said Lloyd W. was jake.

The weather is jake. We have had quite a bit of rain + a little hail but it is very warm + the crops look fine.

Well must say so long for now + will write again soon.

As ever,
Hugh
Can Corps Surv. Sit
France

There were reports regarding food rationing. No hoarding of sugar is allowed. The limit is 2 pounds per month. The province is divided into 7 districts, each with a supervisor. A big fuss was made when E. Curson of Coleville was raided by the Provincial Police. He was fined $100 for having too much sugar.

September 1918

The September 6th paper noted that women cannot wear khaki clothing, even imitations. The military will enforce the rule with fines up to $50. It seems there are more inspectors checking up on us. I guess the worst would be a woman clothed in Khaki concealing large amounts of sugar!

More on sugar – the Food Board seized 12 tons of sugar from Saskatoon Pure Milk Co. They make ice cream. The paper said they were negotiating the fine! Certainly would be more than the $100 amount Curson of Coleville had to pay. The restaurants are allowed more if canning fruit. They cannot use any on fresh fruit. Also, they have to report the amount they use to the Food Board in Ottawa.

We received a wonderful letter from Bill. He sounds more like his old self!

France
Sept 3rd, 1918

Dear Dad

Your long looked for letter arrived at last. The mail has been greatly delayed and it has been rotten waiting. Mais c'est la guerre. The letter I got from you was the one you wrote on Communion Sunday after you had played truant from S.S.

The first part of your letter was very intimate and comforting to me. Do you know, I think you had a great deal of pleasure when you were young, because you had a permanent home. We wanderers had a life about as much like yours, as our home life is like yours on the road. But in your letter I can see that Saskatoon is becoming a real home to you and that the little church is now a permanent part of your life and not only one of many. I think that is why the memories seemed so intimate and sweet.

Last Sunday Dr. Oliver preached the only sermon I had heard preached under a roof for months. It was a tin roof. The music was a concertina, but for peppy singing, that crowd was hard to beat. It reminded me of old Knox Church when Saskatoon was mostly male and mostly from 20 to 30.

The war is going great just now and the end may come soon, who knows. Had a letter from Hugh after a couple of months silence. Characteristically, he ends by saying "will write soon. As always, Hugh" However, if time is short and envelopes are shorter, I don't blame him in using both for the home mail. Today is the first time I have been able to get more than one or two at a time. I have a dozen and about thirty people to write to.

Am sorry to hear that your political views have lost you a few friends but I will trust your judgment and instinct especially as the old party no longer needs anyone's support, anyway, what's the use of getting sore about an opinion, everybody has 'em and they are mostly different.

Tolerance of others honest convictions and unheated discussions seem to me to be only reasonable.

Am sorry the crops are poor but no doubt the farmers will be O.K. and as everyone else is more or less Hooverized, local conditions are more or less compensated for.

For common sense candor and good principles, hand it to the Yanks. I am more or less a Yank myself.

My ideal of the past is Lincoln, of today, Wilson and you know my favourite authors.

Well Dad, for this time, goodbye.

Your son and Pal
Billy

October 1918

There are certain days in one's life that one always remembers.

In today's paper, the Collegiate reported they have 616 pupils and space is critical. There was a special note of praise for the father of Geordie's friend Fred Whittaker. We are "particularly pleased in the way the janitor, A. P. Whittaker, had prepared the building during the summer months for the opening of the school. Much appreciation is expressed at the direction he has taken."

I was just thinking of a way to include young Fred, as he was made to put in many hours during the summer. Then we received another dreaded telegram.

"Sincerely regret inform you nine one nought eight seven one Pte William McKeith Munro Infantry officially reported admitted 4 General Hospital Dannes Camiers Sept 29Th gunshot wound right shoulder."

It seems so unjust. He spent months recovering last year from his neck wound and now this. I wonder if we will ever get to see him again.

There were vague reports of a special flu. Our mayor, Dr. Young, came from Regina on October 16th. He told us in Saskatoon there was no need to be alarmed. Just the following guidelines for any flu – spray throats, steam with Eucalyptus, stay out of crowds. He mentioned there were 150 cases in Regina and only 1 death.

On October 17th, Moose Jaw closes schools. They have 80 in hospital. Also on October 17th, Saskatoon city council voted to close schools and places of amusement, but Mayor Young said not to worry although there were 32 cases here. The medical officer, Dr. Arthur Wilson was also suggesting the Spanish Flu was nothing to worry about. Our numbers quickly grew to 100.

Wilson says this epidemic is nothing but the old form of influenza or grippe. He further added that the only difference is that it has been given more publicity. However, cases are increasing with some victims dying in less than 24 hours.

On October 20th, the churches were closed. By October 21st, there were 239 cases and two deaths. By October 24th, Moose Jaw had 171 cases in hospital and many more at home.

While some local medical professionals are not taking things seriously, our President of the University, Walter Murray, is. He has put the whole campus under quarantine. He gave students and staff one window of opportunity to leave campus. The exception was

Emmanuel College, which he offered as a hospital. Many female volunteers have offered help.

I am very worried. With schools closed, we all try to stay close to home. The girls and I did a lot of extra housecleaning and Jim and George cleaned the basement and the attic. They washed all the outside of windows while the girls did the inside. We also sewed some new skirts. We would have loved to do baking but due to the sugar ration, we could not. We did make oak cakes as they don't use much sugar.

Oh yes – I almost forgot to save a letter we received from Hugh. It arrived October 14th.

France
Oct 4- 1918

Dear Dad
Just a note to say Hello + was very glad to get your letter the last week.
What do you think of the war news now. I wonder if you have as many rumours there as we do here. All the troops are in great spirits or hoping to see the war over before another year.

I saw Billie about a week ago he was Jake. I am going to look him up again as soon as I can.

I was sorry to hear about Willie Drysdale. He did not have a very long time in France did he?

Have you seen John since he got his uniform?

Had a letter from Lulu last night. She says Rossie is taking a steno's course + is going to Calif. too. Cora Thompson + Glady Hay are also going. I wonder what the big attraction is? More men perhaps.

Well news is scarce + I owe many letters so I'll say good night for now.

Best Love to all.
As ever,
Hugh
Can Corps Survey Sect. BEF
France

I was looking back in some newspapers to just before we got the telegram about Bill.

On October 7th, the paper reported Saskatchewan's share of Victory Bonds is 14 – 20 million dollars. The total for Canada is between $420 – $500 million.

Harold Blair was killed. Hugh mentioned him in his June 25th letter. Hugh will be very upset.

The October 8th paper reported 10's of thousands of flu cases in Toronto and 200 thousand in Buenos Aires. Those places seem so far away. According to the same day paper, 2 cases were in the city. I missed noticing that.

On October 12th, a group of Saskatoon men retuning from war was held up in Regina due to flu infections. There were 120 altogether so they were quarantined for a week in the coaches. I still did not really take notice.

November 11, 1918

Another day to remember! There had been rumours that the war was coming to an end. Our phone started to ring very early – in fact at about 3 am. Arch started yelling and we all were awakened. By about 6 am, one caller said how people were celebrating downtown. Our first inclination was to hurry downtown, but Arch said he wasn't comfortable because of the risk of catching the Spanish flu. He decided to go alone and be very careful. He came home in time for supper and shared all that went on.

November 12, 1918

Today's paper had the whole story. I am saving the whole copy as it is full of such details.

"The apartment blocks surrounding the Phoenix office were the first to realise that something unusual had happened when the first racket of peace celebration started at 1 a.m. Monday morning. The entire Phoenix staff turned out with anything and everything available in the shape of a noise producer." Some of the staff used these noise makers and they paraded around the block.

"Cars snorted and honked out of garages . . . and Second avenue buzzed with the thickening traffic."

"For a "dry" town there was considerable moisture." "Chief Donald winked a metaphoric wink at many irregularities."

"Two big bonfires were started on Second Avenue. One of these fires was so successful that Chief Heath thought it advisable to pass out a cooling stream on its ardor."

"The formal celebration procession commenced on Monday afternoon at 2 p.m. It formed on Spadina Crescent with the retuned men lining up outside the G.W.V.A. on 21st Street. Chief Heath led the way, followed by the hook and ladder and the hose cart. Then came the returned soldiers and the Salvation army band with endless cars and trucks filled with cheering crowds bringing up the rear."

"By nine o'clock last night the second evening's rejoicing was in full swing. The ancient and honorable 'See Saskatoon First' bus was pressed into service and oozing citizens at every window and door dashed up and down the street, a very impressive four-in-hand with Kaiser Bill suspended from a pole at the rear. Later on he went up in smoke."

December 1918

November was terrible month for the flu. Emmanuel College at the University set up an emergency hospital. They had 103 cases, mostly nursed by volunteers. The decision to keep the schools closed until January 1919 was made.

A few days before November 11th, there was a report that Germany is near financial ruin. Debts have piled up and their national obligations are over six billion dollars. Germany will have lost over two-thirds of their nation's wealth.

The terms of the Armistice were disclosed

- Evacuation of all occupied territories within 14 days

- Allies to take position on the Rhine

- Must surrender in good condition, 5,000 guns, 30,000 machine guns, 2,000 aeroplanes, 3,000 minenwerfers (trench mortars), 160 submarines, 10 battle cruisers, 6 cruisers, stores of food and ammunitions, 5,000 locomotives, 10,000 lorries and all stores of coal.

On December 5th, the Collegiate report was printed. There are 707 pupils and another high school is needed. The 1st year has 8 Forms totalling 285 pupils. Year 2 has 6 Forms for a total of 218. Year 3 has 4 Forms with 164 pupils. And year 4 has 48 Seniors. The Collegiate has 23 teachers.

A welcome report says food rationing is ending, except for sugar. Restaurants are cautions to still go easy. A big headline was "EAT AS MUCH BREAD AS YOU LIKE!" After being careful for four years, I hope people will practice self-control. I worry about Arch's consumption. However French and puffed pastries must be made with vegetable oils, not animal fats.

Jim and George went to see "20,000 Leagues Under the Sea" by Jules Verne. It took two years to make the film and cost ½ million dollars. They were so excited they took us all back the next day to see it.

Moose Jaw Museum had an exhibit of war trophies taken at Flanders Fields. Five carloads of trophies and photos came direct from the battle fields. The display was on from December 14th to 21st. Arch and Jim went by train to see it. Admission was 25¢ for adults and 10¢ for children.

On December 18th we got a letter from Hugh.

Germany

Dear Mother

Received quite a bundle of letters from home a few days ago and was glad to hear the flu has not got any of you! There isn't very much of it here for some reason – everyone else seems to get it. We crossed the frontier yesterday, so are now in Germany or West Prussia. I don't think there can be much German Army left as all the men seem to be ex-soldiers.

On December 12th the paper said 23,000 Saskatchewan men will stay in Europe for up to eighteen months longer.

McCarthy Jewellers is going out of business. Arch spotted the sale and insisted we get each girl a Waltham watch. They were regular $30 but on sale for $13.77 each. They will be their Christmas gifts. We want them to be a sign for the years ahead, full of hope and joy. The young people must look forward. To look back serves no purpose.

There was a report about the Eskimos on Seward Peninsula. There are a great number of flu cases. In Nome alone there were 156 cases. About a half dozen villages were wiped out except for some children who seem to be spared. In Quebec there were ½ million cases with 13,880 deaths reported. The Saskatchewan death toll stands at over 2,000.

My preparations for Christmas this year are better than last. We are inviting my brother James and his wife Kate to supper on the 24th. We haven't seen them for quite some time. Caroline and Helen should have a good time although they see one another at school. We are anxious to hear Caroline play the piano. She has been in several piano recitals. Mack will get our Geordie going. Mack is an imp, but a loveable one. Church on Christmas Day will be special. We have many things to give thanks for.

January 1919

All our spirits are brighter. Although the boys didn't make it home for Christmas, we didn't have to worry as much.

Oh yes – Arch surprised me with a watch also. He bought it at McCarthy's sale. It was extra special. A 23 carat Elgin. (I remember – on sale for $65!)

On January 6 we received a letter from Hugh. He never seems to get down in spirits, but always seems cheery.

Wanhnerheile
Dec 22-1918

Dear Mother,
    No mail from home this week but Canadian mail has arrived so am looking for some soon. We are

nearly settled in our new home and like it very well have a comfortable room four of us + the Germans supply lots of coal so we are jake.

Was down to Cologne the other night + had a pretty good time we were in the Cathedral it is supposed to be one of the finest in the world and it certainly is nice. I'll send you a picture of it some of these days.

Only three days till Xmas and I'll be on guard till 4 p.m. Xmas but that's better than having to go on at 4 Xmas day and miss the shindig. We are having a dinner, and on the 26th a concert. We didn't have very much time to get ready but are going to have as good a time as possible anyway.

One of the fellows is going on leave tomorrow. His home is in England and he will arrive there Xmas day or the day before.

How is the flu getting along. I hope it is all over by now.

Had a parcel from Westminster a few days ago will reply after Xmas. Mrs. Carle packed It up + put a note on it.

Do you or the girls know a Miss Shiers who teaches in Victoria school. I think she has a class at

Westminster too and rooms with Miss Little. Her brother is in the CCSS + in the same room with me.
Will need to close now.

With best love to all,
As ever
Hugh

I was thinking of the message given by Rev. Wylie Clark so many years ago. He talked about the fear of not remembering. Sometimes I worry as I am starting to forget little things I should remember. My family has a history of forgetting some things and becoming senile. Rev. Clark also talked about the fear of being forgotten. I wonder if anyone will remember me. I feel great sadness when I think about people who die and are soon forgotten. I hope there are people who will remember the lads that died in the war. I honour the memory of my father. He was such a loving father. Will there be anyone who remembers me after I have died?

Oh dear! I just covered the last page in this journal. I wish I had started a brand new journal with this last entry. I should copy this into my new journal. This year, more than any other, we can start fresh. The war is finally over. 1919 has such a nice ring to it!

Epilogue - 2022

Belle Munro faithfully recorded the events in her life for many years. Arch died in 1933 and it was evident she could not stay alone in the house. While sorting out the contents of 422 9th Street, Nan and Helen carefully put the rest of her journals in a box to be saved. For over 30 years the arguments continued as to whether George or Jim had accidently thrown them out.

Gradually Belle became more confused, having early onset dementia. She lived with George and Jim at Rosetown and then with Hugh at the farm. She made visits down East to Nan's and Helen's.

George took over her affairs and was a devoted son. When George enlisted in World War II, he made arrangements for her to live in a private care home. When George returned home, he bought a house on University Drive that suited her needs for a while. George taught at The Tech but it became unsafe for her to be alone in the daytime hours. He placed his mother in North Battleford Mental Institute in 1953. She died in 1955. She was eighty-nine years old.

Memories of Grandma Belle

I haven't any early memories. The fist memory is from 1941. My Uncle Jim brought her to visit just before he went overseas as a Chaplain. I was only five and I couldn't quite understand that I had another grandmother.

My maternal grandmother, Grandma Muzzy, played a huge part in my life. My concept of a grandmother was one who was tall and substantial, who was strong, opinionated, and very practical. This grandma was petite and soft spoken.

During the war years, my Uncle George also went overseas. He was the main caregiver, so he made arrangements for Grandma Belle to stay in a private home on Avenue E North. Mrs. Ireland was just the right person to care for her. A few times my sister Win and I went to visit her. She was polite, but obviously did not recognize us. We would say we were Bill's daughters and her face would light up for a few seconds. Mrs.

Ireland had to ask my mother to stop letting us visit because for a few days after a visit Grandma would be restless and she would slip out of the house and wander.

The Vice-Principal at Bedford was Mr. MacLennan. He started his teaching career at Nutana Collegiate circa 1918 and had taught my aunts Nan and Helen. He finished his teaching career at Bedford in 1954. He knew the Munro family and would spot Grandma outside. He would call my older sister Isabel and she would come and take Grandma home, much to the relief of Mrs. Ireland.

In retrospect, I notice the distance from Avenue E and Bedford was about the same distance and con-figuration as the walk from 422 9th Street to Nutana Collegiate. She seemed to be searching for someone, usually her youngest son Geordie.

When George came home from the war, he bought a house on University Drive. That suited her needs. Uncle George was teaching at Tech, but devoted time to Grandma. He took her for walks, especially on Broadway and along the riverbank. He bought her new dresses and kept her beautiful snowy white hair carefully waved. He took her to Church, read to her and sang hymns and Scottish songs.

Well done little "Geordie Mack"!

On December 6, 1946 my father, her eldest son, died in the Barry Hotel Fire. I was at Parkview Presbyterian Church and George and Jim came for me and took me home. There were several fractures in our family so my mother chose not to attend his funeral. My sister Isabel had to identify our father's body and of course she was distraught. I remember my mixed feelings. There seemed to be so many relatives present that I did not know. Yet I remember thinking, "I _am_ a Munro, part of a larger family. I remember my sister Isabel crying and I did not, but I felt guilty that I was not as upset as she was. They did not bring Grandma to the funeral as they thought it would be too upsetting.

One of my strongest memories of Grandma Belle is the gathering at Uncle George's after the funeral. Her other five children and some close friends were present. I remember how Grandma was sitting in the comfortable cane-backed Eastlake chair. She seemed pleased that the gathering seemed like a party to her. Her eyes became clear and her face lit up. She pointed to her daughter Nan and exclaimed "Nan it is you! What a surprise!" Then, in turn, she pointed to Hugh, Jim, George and Helen. Everyone was excited. Then she said, "Too bad Willie couldn't make it!" Stunned silence! No one wanted say he was dead.

To break the awkward silence, Uncle George took my arm and led me over to her chair saying, "Look Mother, this is Bill's youngest daughter." She opened her arms and insisted I sit on her lap. I was afraid I would squash her so I tried to brace myself on the arms of the chair. She hugged and hugged me, rocking, calling me "her darling baby". As she calmed down, her bright eyes dimmed.

Physically, she had clear, bright blue eyes that I called crinkly. The seemed to sparkle. Her snowy white hair was always the same soft curls close to her head. She had lovely dresses and her favourites were often trimmed with lace collars. She always wore a broach, but always at the centre of her dress – never on her shoulder. She had many fine necklaces given to her by her husband Arch and her children. She loved looking at all her jewellry and sometimes she would hide a piece in a "safe place" and then become agitated as she thought it had been stolen.

Another interesting thing about my grandmother is that for years she had a condition called essential tremors, also known as the "shakes". Her head always gently, rhythmically, shook up and forward, not side to side. With a pleasant smile on her face, I liked to think she was saying "yes, yes, yes". She presented to me the perfect picture of a gracious, fragile, special person.

In the earlier days with dementia, she seemed to be aware and she chose not to speak much. If she thought she had made a mistake, she would be very embarrassed and upset with herself and would become silent.

My Muzzy side consisted of my mother, grandmother, two aunts, two cousins, my two sisters and me. They gave me stability and the practical necessities of life, like a place to live, food and handmade clothes. They were not prone to hugging, let alone kissing.

I found the Munro side somewhat mysterious and intriguing. They loved smart clothes, fine jewellry and rich food. They hugged and kissed and laughed together. I treasure both sides for very different reasons.

The Church

Arch and Belle were stanch Presbyterians. When the family came to Saskatoon in 1908. The six children went to the original Knox Church by the river. Later they were members of Westminster Presbyterian Church in Nutana. Arch loved to teach Sunday school.

For several years, some members of the Methodist, Presbyterian and Congregationalist denominations wanted to amalgamate and form a new church. Each congregation had one vote and a congregation had to opt out of joining, a fact that was withheld from many members. Very abruptly, Knox, Westminster and St. Thomas Churches voted to join the Union. The church buildings and all assets became the property of the newly formed United Church. Many members did not agree with the decision and found they had lost everything that so many had helped build.

Thus, 1925 became a very important year in Presbyterian history.

Archie Munro went into action! He called the first meeting to form a new Presbyterian congregation. This group became known informally as "the continuing Presbyterians". A hall was rented, the call went out and in a matter of days, 384 people joined!

Arch was elected as a first Elder. He had a lot of help and guidance from his brother Rev. Donald Munro of North Battleford. The new Church put out a "call" to a very well-known minister, Rev. G. W. Brown of Red Deer. The name St. Andrew's was chosen. The new congregation was built around the personality and charisma of Rev. Brown.

A "basement" church was built on 4th Avenue. They established Sunday school in several schools and flourished. Arch and son Jim Munro were Sunday School teachers. Jim, originally a teacher, felt "the Call" and became a Presbyterian minister.

Rev. Brown had a weekly radio program. He published a magazine called "The Blue Banner". He was also politically active. He was a founding member of the United Reform Party. He was elected as a Member of Parliament, but ill health overtook him, and he died in 1931.

Jim Munro delivered the funeral address. Bill Munro wrote political speeches for Rev. Brown.

In 1953, the new St. Andrew's was built on Spadina Crescent. Rev. Jim Munro laid the cornerstone and preached the first sermon. Three generations of Munros, over 75 years, have been Elders in the congregation: Archie Munro, his son George Munro and Archie's granddaughter, Margaret Munro.

Population of Saskatoon

	1901	1911	1921	1931	1941
Population		12,004	25,739	43,291	43,027
East	179				
West	306				
Scottish	105	2,695	5,985	8,815	8,237

Religious Affiliations in Saskatoon

Presbyterian*	186	3,101	7,870	5,310	4,407
R. Catholic	59	1,110	2,883	6,551	6,907
Anglican	73	3,212	7,473	10,313	10,042
Methodist*	153	2,368	3677	0	0
Baptist	3	608	892	1,463	1,304
Lutheran	0	310	625	1,770	1,692
United*	0	0	0	13,501	13,902
Jewish	0	76	599	688	685

- Note: The decline in the number of Presbyterians and Methodists reflects the union of many of their congregations and the resulting emergence of the United Church in 1925.

In 1911, approximately 31 percent of the population identified as Presbyterian. In 1921, Presbyterians were approximately 30 percent of the population. By 1931, the percentage had dropped to eight. In 1941, approximately nine percent of the population identified as Presbyterian.

The Clan Munro

Archibald Munro
March 29, 1864 – September 6,1933
Isabella (Belle) Munro (Born a Stewart)
December 20, 1865 – February 6, 1955

What happened to their children?

George (Geordie) McLeod Munro
October 30, 1904 – December 17, 1969

George was a teacher at Tech after World War II

He became Principal of Nutana Collegiate, a
source of pride, as that was the High School he
had attended

He was 65 years old when he died of heart failure

Helen Margaret Munro
November 25, 1902 – December 7, 1987

Helen taught school in several one-room schools
throughout Saskatchewan

In 1931, Helen married Reid Elliott
(April 19, 1904 – April 11, 1974)

Their children

Robert Archie Elliott
August 7, 1931 – October 8, 2008

Dale Margaret Elliott
December 17, 1934

Gary Neil Elliott
May 30, 1943 – October 16, 2009

Nan Lovina Elliott
August 4, 1944

Nan Kathleen Munro
May 1, 1900 – February 9, 1983

In 1927, Nan married Joseph (Joe) Wilhelm
(July 16, 1899 – November 19, 1953)

Their children

Donald Alan Wilhelm
June 27, 1928 – November 30, 1998

Mildred Isabel Wilhelm

July 29, 1937 – November 13, 2018

James Alan Munro

July 4, 1898 – June 18, 1972

Jim was first a teacher and then became a Minister in the Presbyterian Church in Canada

He served as a chaplain in World War II and was wounded at the front and received the Military Cross as well as being mentioned in several dispatches

He was Moderator of the Presbyterian Church in Canada in 1965

Hugh Archibald Munro

January 29, 1897 – December 11, 1951

Hugh taught school and then became the much loved Postmaster at Marsden, Saskatchewan

William (Willie, Billie or Bill) McKeith Munro

July 2, 1895 – December 8, 1946

Bill studied law and then taught school at several locations

Because of Shellshock and depression, he often had to resign

In 1926 he married Vera Muzzy
(March 10, 1900 – January 2, 1966)

Bill died in the Barry Hotel fire on December 8, 1946

Their children

Helen Isabel Munro
December 25, 1926 – January 21, 2014

Nan Winnifred Munro
February 21, 1934

Frances Margaret Munro
April 18, 1936

Belle and Archie had six children, nine grandchildren and twenty-nine great-grandchildren.

Willie and Hugh Munro 1897.

Jim and Nan Munro 1901.

Nan, Helen, Willie, Geordie and Jim Munro in a picture taken by their brother Hugh.